Drifting

SIDEWAYS FROM JAPAN TO AMERICA

ANTONIO ALVENDIA

CIPHER GARAGE

MOTORBOOKS

DEDICATION

To my little brother David. Don't waste any opportunity to do something that drives you. Think big.
If you stay motivated and have passion for what you're doing, you can do anything.

To drifters and drifting enthusiasts all over the world. Drifting is not a passing fad. Drifting is our heart. Drifting is our lifestyle.
Drifting is our culture, and it has changed our lives forever. This book was made for you. Never stop drifting.

First published in 2006 by Motorbooks, an imprint of MBI Publishing Company, Galtier Plaza, Suite 200, 380 Jackson Street, St. Paul, MN 55101-3885 USA

MBI Publishing Company titles are also available at discounts in bulk quantity for industrial or sales-promotional use. For details write to Special Sales Manager at MBI Publishing Company, Galtier Plaza, Suite 200, 380 Jackson Street, St. Paul, MN 55101-3885 USA

Library of Congress Cataloging-in-Publication Data

Alvendia, Antonio.
   Drifting : sideways from Japan to America / Antonio Alvendia.
      p. cm.
   Includes bibliographical references and index.
   ISBN-13: 978-0-7603-2417-2
      (hardcover : alk. paper)
   ISBN-10: 0-7603-2417-4 (hardcover : alk. paper)
   1. Drifting (Motorsport)--United States.   I. Title.

GV1029.9.D75A59 2006
 796.72--dc22

On the front cover: Chris Forsberg maneuvers his SR20DET-powered Nissan 350 Z at Drift Showoff at Irwindale Speedway, California.

On the back cover: *(top left)* Nobuteru Taniguchi (red JZS161 Aristo/Lexus GS) and Rhys Millen (yellow Pontiac GTO) perform a drift demo at the Long Beach Grand Prix.
(top middle) Justin Kikkawa from Hawaii's Drift Session is the perfect example of a hardcore drifter with heart.
*(bottom middle)*Falken Umbrella Girls
(top right) Rhys Millen and JR Gittin tandem match at Road Atlanta.
*(bottom right)*Robbie Nishida vs. Samuel Hubinette at Wall Speedway, New Jersey.

About the author: Antonio Alvendia is a freelance photographer and writing who lives in the Los Angeles area. A lifelong Japanese car enthusiast, he has been involved in the U.S. drifting scene since its emergence.

Editor: Jennifer Johnson
Designer: Brenda C. Canales
Cover Design: Mark Arcenal of www.arcenal.com

Printed in China

Disclaimer:
Drifting can be a dangerous motorsport. The drivers depicted in this book are all professionals. Attempting to duplicate their actions may be hazardous. Readers are cautioned that individual abilities, cars, tracks, roads, and driving conditions differ, and due to these unlimited factors beyond the control of the author and drivers quoted in this book, liability is expressly disclaimed. Do not attempt any maneuvers, stunts, or techniques that are beyond your capabilities.

Contents

"It was all a dream, I used to read Battle Magazine..."

Friday, April 28, 2006 5:55 p.m.

As I write this, I'm sitting on a jetplane somewhere high above the Pacific Ocean, on my way to Japan for my annual pilgrimage to the Holy Land of drifting. Once I arrive in Tokyo, I'll take the *shinkansen* (bullet train) to Ebisu Circuit, where I'll meet up with my close friends, Nobushige Kumakubo, Kazuhiro Tanaka, and Naoto Suenaga—also known as Team Orange, the top tandem drifting team in the world.

The next day, I'll ride with them to the D1 Round at Sugo Raceway, the first D1 event I will have ever experienced in Japan. Two days after D1 Sugo is the annual Harumatsuri Drifting Festival at Ebisu, where the people at Ebisu celebrate the falling sakura flowers (cherry blossoms) and the coming of the spring with a festival of drifting that lasts for 36 hours. Drivers come from all over Japan every year to participate, with an average of 700 drift cars registered and ready to drive by 10:00 a.m. on the day of the festival. Ebisu's Harumatsuri Festival is not a festival for spectators; it is a festival for the drivers—the real heart of Ebisu Circuit.

Two days after Harumatsuri is the annual Big X Festival—the first fusion of drifting into other extreme action sports—where top drifters of Japan drive in synchronization with stunt drivers, who launch their cars sideways (on two wheels) on the racetrack, in tandem with stunt bike riders doing wheelies and endos. The drifters speed through the track in a 7-car tandem procession, slaloming around the moving group of stunt cars and bike riders, as freestyle motocross riders jump high over the track.

After Big X, I will return to my home in Los Angeles for less than 12 hours, just to fly out again the next morning for Formula D Round 2, in the dirty south: Atlanta Georgia.

This is my life. Rather than write the typical author's introduction, of how I got started into photography, and how I fell in love with drifting, I thought I would instead tell the story of how I'm choosing to live my life right now—the drifting life. On the eve of my book's deadline, with all the pressure of last-minute editing and layout, compounded with the fact that I now need to make an international call from Japan with a 14 hour time difference just to work on the book layout with my editor at MBI, I still feel at this moment, that I couldn't be doing anything more important than this. It is the unforgettable experience like this that keeps me going and keeps me motivated.

This is, after all, the lifestyle I chose to live. Not many other people are presented with an opportunity to do what they love, so I would be foolish not to jump at the chance like this. To me, it's like living out a dream.

Just a few years ago, I used to look at photos of my favorite cars and drivers in Japanese drifting magazines, but today, I've become close personal friends with many of the people I idolized when I was first getting into drifting.

Drifting has brought me all over the United States and Japan. I've shot photos everywhere from "the house that drifting built," Southern California's Irwindale Speedway, to Ebisu Circuit, "the Holy Land of drifting." I've enjoyed the cool breeze and aloha attitude of Drift Session in Hawaii, I've witnessed Japan's top privateers drifting at the BM Cup at Tsukuba Circuit, and I've even experienced hanging Vietnam-style out of a helicopter at the Pike's Peak International Hillclimb, with nothing more than a shiesty lap belt to prevent me from plummeting to the ground. I mean, you get at least a 3-point belt, even when you're sitting in a car, but I was dangling precariously out of a helicopter, higher than 10,000 feet above sea level, and it was freezing. It's been quite a journey. Through my travels, I've built several close friendships that I value greatly, but what will never cease to amaze and inspire me are the drivers in all the different parts of the world who share the same passion for drifting.

To me, drifting is not just a passing fad. Drifting has completely changed my life. Drifting *is* my life. I've put my whole heart into my photos of drifting, and now I'm opening it up to you in the pages of this book. This project means a lot to me. After all, this has been my whole life for the past few years.

During the last few years, my life has been dedicated entirely to the pursuit of drifting and drifting photography. I've dedicated my life to following the cars, drivers, and teams around the world, documenting the emergence of drifting in the United States, and how it evolved from being just a bunch of young kids having fun driving their cars at the limit to the rapidly growing motorsports lifestyle it is today.

Nowadays, drifting has become big business. What was once an underground motorsport has blown up faster than many of us expected. Drifting is now seen on nationwide television, in magazines, in major video games, in die-cast toys, on trading cards, and in major motion pictures. Now companies outside the auto industry are starting to look at drifting as a viable way to reach the elusive youth market. Even a company such as Red Bull, who sponsors Formula 1, has entered into the scene, sponsoring one of the top teams in American professional drifting. Drifting will continue to grow, but that's only if we continue to support drifters on the amateur level, and most importantly, the people who organize the grassroots drifting events. After all,

it is those people who are building new drifters and teaching them how to drive.

This goes out to all the drifters and drifting enthusiasts out there. This book is for you and about you. Support the drifting movement. Stay passionate about drifting, and never stop.

Antonio Alvendia
Cipher Garage

By Calvin Wan

Drifting has changed my life dramatically. It has given me the opportunity to experience driving many different types of cars, and has led me to travel across the world. Because of drifting, I have been given the opportunity to be a stunt driver for a major motion picture- Fast and Furious: Tokyo Drift. Drifting has opened many doors for me to be directly involved in professional driving. Drifting has become the "extreme sport" of the automotive industry, It has brought new life and attention to motor sports in the United States, as well as many other countries around the world. My first exposure to drifting was watching Option videos in the early to mid-1990s. The first time I saw drifting, I remember thinking how cool the cars looked going sideways through turns. I was so fascinated by this unique driving style—I started to take interest in everything drift related! I remember watching clips of *Initial D* and playing Tokyo Highway Battle (which was all about drifting) on Playstation. and I was so intrigued with how big drifting was in Japan.

I met Antonio in the late 1990s in the San Francisco Bay Area. We both had AE86s at the time, and we started a group called the AE86 Driving Club. We met up every weekend at a local restaurant, or at Graphtech (a graphics shop I co-founded), talked about AE86s for hours, and then drove in the canyons.

Antonio was with me during my early experiences with drifting. When we first started the AE86 Club, we went to the local canyon roads and found a good corner where everyone parked their cars on the shoulders and shined their headlights onto the road. We took turns drifting thecorner. We only went to the mountains because there weren't any organized drift events at the time—there was just no where else to drift.

My first experience drifting a real car was in 1996, and I have been hooked ever since. I've owned rear-wheel-drive cars, including a KP61 Starlet, couple of AE86s, and an E30 M3 that I drifted, here and there. But because there weren't any organized drift events in America at that time, I concentrated more on racing—competing in autocrosses, rally crosses, and road races.

It wasn't until 2002 that regular, sanctioned drift events finally started popping up in California—I was so excited that there were finally legitimate events where I could practice drifting. From then on, I shifted my focus to drifting; and drove at every single drift event in California. I drove a 1993 RX-7 at the time, and with that car, I developed my drifting technique. I became heavily involved with the sport and became a Drift Association instructor. In 2003 I became one of the first Americans to qualify for the Inaugural D1 Grand Prix in the USA—a definite highlight in my drifting career.

U.S. drifting really kicked off in 2003. Drift competitions started popping up all over Southern California. There still weren't any regular drift events in Northern California at the time, and since my hometown is San Francisco, I had to drive down to SoCal as often as three times a month to make it to all the drift events.

The costs of constantly trailering my car to LA and paying to drive at events really added up, but Antonio was kind enough to let me stay at his place in So Cal all the time.

In 2004, I became Falken Tire's first American team driver, driving the Falken/Discount Tire–sponsored S13 240SX. I competed in the inaugural season of the Formula Drift Championship, achieving a podium placing and finishing fourth overall for the season. I also began driving in drifting demonstrations throughout the country at Drift Showoff events and Formula D's Champ Car Demos, as well as judging drifting events for several different drifting organizations around the country.

In 2005, I became the first person in the world to drive an Infiniti G35 / Skyline CPV35 in a professional drift competition. With the G35, I became the first driver in Formula D history to win 1st Place in an import car. All of the previous 1st Place wins had been in American cars.

I wasn't the only one whose life was affected so much by drifting. Antonio went to all of the events with me to shoot photos. He was the only photographer who was involved from the very beginning, when the whole drifting movement started. Most photographers just showed up to select events here and there, but Antonio documented *every* event, whether it was a Drift Day or a D1.

As a photographer, Antonio created his own style of shooting. He was able to create more excitement in drifting photography with distinctive angles; he had a sharp eye for what looked good. But most of all, what truly sets him apart from all other photographers and writers out there, is that he really is passionate about drifting culture. His passion for "living the 86 life," or AE86 lifestyle, is unmatched by any other person I've met. He has an impressive collection of AE86-chassis Corollas, along with all the drifting memorabilia and rare parts to go with the cars in his collection. He is well connected with many key industry people worldwide.

Antonio's strong passion for drifting culture, his insider knowledge, and his complete collection of drifting photography make him the ideal person to write the first book on drifting in America. He has been there every step of the way, shooting photos of the drifting scene as it evolved, and as I developed my career as a driver.

Drifting has become a lifestyle for me, and I see it becoming a lifestyle for so many others in the future. It's a motorsport that's here to stay. What follows here is its first photographic record in book form.

WHAT IS DRIFTING?

Ichigo Battle! A pair of S15 Nissan Silvias—driven by drifting legends Nobushige Kumakubo (leading, in the Team Orange S15) and Nobuteru Taniguchi (in the red HKS S15)—duke it out in front of a packed house at "the house that drifting built," Irwindale Speedway, during a D1 top-8 competition.

Drifting can be described as "controlled chaos," or the art of controlling a vehicle that is seemingly out of control. To the average onlooker, drifting is nothing more than mere oversteer—applying too much throttle so the car loses traction while negotiating the turns. Wrong! There is a lot more to drifting than simply mashing the gas pedal to get the tail end of the car sideways.

In actuality, drifting is a driving style in which the driver uses the throttle, brakes, clutch, gear shifting, and steering input to keep the car in a condition of oversteer while maneuvering from turn to turn. Drifters emphasize car control by coordinating the amount of countersteer with the simultaneous modulation of the throttle and brakes to shift the weight balance of the car back and forth through the turns. Furthermore, they strive to achieve this while adhering to the standard racing lines and maintaining extreme slide angles.

WHY DRIFT?

Road racing traditionalists are often quick to point out that drifting is not the fastest way around a racetrack, and they're right. But so what? When drifters drive on the racetrack or on a twisty mountain road, what usually matters most is having fun! There is something inherently exciting about driving on a road course, negotiating turns with the car crossed up, quickly countersteering in the direction of the slide while delicately modulating pressure on the throttle. Not enough throttle, and the car will lose the momentum of the drift. Too much throttle and the car ends up in a spin.

Some drivers really like the fact that drifting practice events teach them how to control a car that's at its limits. It allows them to safely lose control of the car, and then regain that control of it. Others just enjoy the thrill and adrenaline rush involved in the sideways momentum of a high-speed, tire-shredding drift. In its simplest sense, drifting translates to pure driving enjoyment.

DRIFTING COMPETITION

It has been said that being a spectator at a drifting competition is like capturing the most exhilarating moments of the most exciting road racing event you've ever watched in your life, and then seeing it take place live, over and over again. Competitive drifting is a motorsport judged on style and execution, not on the amount of time it takes to get through the course. In this way, drifting is akin to freestyle surfing, motocross, or skateboarding. It isn't about top speed or crossing the checkered flag first. Instead, drifting is a performance-oriented motorsport in which the objective is to put on a great show for the judges and spectators.

A pair of AE86 Corolla Levins from famed AE86 drift team T50 Japan (Go-Maru Japan) stick close together during the team drifting competition of *Battle Magazine's* BM Cup Series (BM Hi). This photo was shot during the last year of the BM Hi Series at the Tsukuba Circuit in Ibaragi, Japan where T50 Japan won first place in the team drifting competition.

JUDGING DRIFTING

In evaluating a driver's performance, drifting is judged on four main factors: speed, line, angle, and showmanship.

As far as speed goes, judges award higher points for higher entry speed when a driver comes into a turn. Higher entry speed shows not only

Tandem drifting pioneer and Japanese drifting legend Nobushige Kumakubo of Team Orange accelerates right after the course's transition point on Irwindale Speedway's banked oval, creating a high-speed smokescreen with his S15 Silvia's Advan Neova tires. As only an experienced eye can tell, the high speed of the car is apparent in the way smoke comes off the rear tires. Slower drifting speeds result in thicker, billowing clouds of smoke; higher speeds result in thinner, vapor-like smoke.

Known for driving his A31 Nissan Cefiro 4-door sedan, Michihiro Takatori is one of the top drivers from a drift team in Kyoto, Japan called Heaven.

guts, but the level of the driver's commitment on the entry. Overall speed throughout the entire course is also a factor.

The drivers are also judged on how well they adhere to the driving line. Drifters follow a line that is very similar to the driving lines used in road racing—the fastest line around the course. On corner entries, the driver should stay as wide as possible, then tuck tight into the apex, hitting the indicated clipping points. (The clipping point is the inside apex; the point where the car touches the inside of the turn.) Hitting the clipping points is watched very strictly by the judges. When exiting the corner, it is best to bring the car out wide to the edge of the track, using the full width of the course. The transition from corner to corner should be smooth so the driver can adhere to the driving line properly.

The degree of the car's slip angle (also referred to as drift angle) is of paramount importance in a drifting competition. More skilled drivers are awarded more points for being able to drift the car at extremely deep angles; the deeper the angle, the higher the likelihood of spinning. Therefore, the deeper the angle, the higher the points and the cooler it looks. Even

Hiroshi Fukuda, from renown drift team Fluke, competes in the D1 Series with his yellow 180SX, which has aggressive aero typical of newer-style pro drift cars. This style became popular because people liked the aggressive, low look of the cars, but it is so low it is impractical for driving on the street! Fukuda, who started drifting because he liked WRC Rally, is from Japan's Tochigi prefecture and often practices drifting at Nikko Circuit.

Living Legends. Finding Japanese racing pioneers like Kunimitsu Takahashi (left) and Keiichi Tsuchiya (right) together to pose for a photo is difficult indeed. Kuni-san (Takahashi) was the inspiration behind Keiichi Tsuchiya's high-speed driving techniques on the racetrack, but it was Keiichi who became known as "the Drift King."

The First Video Option Ikaten Drift Competition in the United States, Willow Springs, 1996

Video Option2, Volume 18 (December 1996) featured the first Option Ikaten (EE-ka-ten) Drift Competition in the United States at Willow Springs Raceway in Rosamond, California in August 1995. For this event, Option's owner, Daijiro Inada, traveled to Southern California with the Drift King, Keiichi Tsuchiya, and popular Option Video star Ken Nomura, or "Nomuken." Option Video hosted the event, and Greddy U.S.A. (the U.S. branch of Trust, one of Japan's top aftermarket tuning companies) and ACE (Amateur Circuit Experience) road racing organizer Tommy Chen helped organize it.

Video Option filmed Keiichi drifting Willow Springs with a new *kouki* (late model) RPS13 Nissan 180SX, the last model of S13 to be sold in Japan. The 180SX was outfitted with parts from Tsuchiya's company, Kei Office, and Tsuchiya took the American novice drifters for rides around the track. Tommy Chen recalls, "Keiichi didn't use the e-brake at all. He just came into each corner hot, and late braked into the corner, and kept the drift going. He was so smooth. I was in awe! That was definitely the most memorable ride-along I ever had."

Some of the amateur drifters competing at this event included Greddy's own Bryan Norris, a hardcore Southern California canyon runner who entered the event with his red AE86 Corolla GT-S. Norris was one of the earliest American fans of underground Japanese drifting and car culture. He went on to partner with Tommy Chen from ACE, and they later formed SpeedTrial USA,

Image Courtesy of Bryan Norris

an organization that welcomed early drifters to their amateur circuit events in Southern California.

Also present at the event was a young Rhys Millen, who was already a sponsored racer. Millen attempted to get the hang of drifting in his silver JZA80 Toyota Supra Turbo, but at that stage of his career, he was not even close to being the professional drifter that he is today.

though drivers seek to attain as much slide angle as possible, it's important to maintain balance along with speed. Often, when the slide angle is too deep, the car slows down. On the other hand, if the driver enters the corner carrying too much speed, it often results in shallow angle. Balance is key!

Last but not least, drifting competition runs are judged on the amount of showmanship the driver demonstrates. Showmanship is based on many criterion, including: the engine screaming as the driver pins the needle to the redline, the clouds of thick tire smoke billowing from the fender wells, how close a driver can get to the wall, the roar of the car's exhaust, the whooshing turbo and wastegate noises, and even the style of the car's aero kit and graphics. The earlier a driver initiates drift, the higher the style points. While the car is in drift, quick, sharp transitions from side to side also add to the excitement of the run. Each driver has their

own individual style and flair. Drifting is an art form, and in the mind of a driver, it is an art form that can become very personal.

In tandem runs, the lead driver sets the pace. It is the goal of the lead driver to drive a perfect line as fast as possible and leave the follower behind. The follower's goal is to follow the lead car's pace as closely as possible, and to outdrive the lead driver by maintaining a close distance to the lead car throughout the course without affecting the lead driver's line.

JAPANESE DRIFTING HISTORY
Kunimitsu Takahashi

In Japan, the first use of drifting as a competition driving technique on paved tarmac surfaces was in

the 1970s. Nissan's KPGC10 Skyline GT-R, affectionately known as the "Hakosuka," or "box-Skyline" won 50 straight races in the All Japan Touring Car Championship in the 1960s and 1970s. This was the first generation of Skyline, and the GT-R badge signified the car was built with the sole purpose of winning races. This first-generation Skyline GT-R competed against the Nissan's B110 Sunny Excellent (Datsun 1200) and P510 Bluebird (Datsun 510); Mazda's S122A RX2 and S124A RX3; and Toyota's TA20 Celica, TE27 Corolla Levin, and TE27 Sprinter Trueno models.

Even back then, some racers drifted as they drove their cars faster and faster around the track, testing the limits of tire adhesion. Nobody drifted on the track as well as Kunimitsu Takahashi, a Japanese racing legend who was famous for all his road racing wins driving his Nissan Works Team KPGC10 Skyline GT-R. As a seasoned racer, Takahashi drove his Hakosuka so hard, he apexed the turns and literally drifted on almost every corner of the track—a technique that worked very well for him, as he won many race events in the All Japan Touring Car Championship and captured several championships over his racing career. He went on to become the chairman of Japan's GT Association, the organization that produces the JGTC, or Super GT, race events around the world.

THE DRIFT KING
Keiichi Tsuchiya

Because of his unique driving style, Takahashi gained a lot of attention from racing enthusiasts and drivers alike. One such enthusiast was Keiichi Tsuchiya. Keiichi, who is also referred to as "the Drift King," or "Dorikin" for short, was an ordinary grassroots street racer when he first attended the races at legendary Mount Fuji Speedway in the 1970s. When Keiichi saw Takahashi's high-speed driving techniques, drifting through the corners while racing, he was completely amazed. Feeling inspired by Takahashi's driving, Keiichi started his career as a professional racing driver and entered the Fuji Freshman Race in 1977. Even though Keiichi started his career in pro racing, he still loved to race and practice his drifting skills on the street. Apparently, as the saying goes, you can take the racer off the streets, but can't take the street out of the racer. Tales of Keiichi's drifting skills on the street spread quickly by word of mouth, and soon almost all the hashiriya (street racers) knew about Keiichi and were greatly interested in seeing him drive.

THE FIRST DRIFTING VIDEO

Not too long after Keiichi rose to prominence, some of the more popular car magazines and tuning garages worked together to produce a video titled *Pluspy (*plus-pee)*, which featured Keiichi drifting his white 1986 AE86 Sprinter Trueno GTV hatchback on a windy mountain road (that most hashiriya refer to as touge (TOW-geh). This initial

Industry Profile: Drift Association—www.driftday.com

Even back when SpeedTrial USA events were the most popular track day events for AE86 owners, Moto Miwa and other AE86 owners would often attend private events at Willow Springs International Raceway hosted by Naoki Kobayashi.

At that time, Naoki was becoming more and more interested in AE86 Corollas since he just bought one himself. Naoki began talking to Moto, picking his brain about Corollas, and eventually they thought up the idea of a drifting clinic for Club4AG members—a day when Corolla drivers could get together to have fun and practice drifting. This drifting clinic would be the first one of its kind.

On March 16, 2002, Moto and Naoki held Drift Day 1, under the name Drift Association. Approximately 45 drivers came out to practice drifting at the Irwindale Speedway parking lot, with close to 150 spectators. Signal Auto brought their cars, and many of Southern California's drifters got a taste of what it would be like to practice drifting legally, without the worry of falling off the side of a cliff, smacking a curb, running into poles, or running from police. Even though it was a small event, large nationwide magazines like Super Street covered the event.

"You know, what I think really makes Drift Association special," Naoki continues, "is that it has hundreds and hundreds of followers and volunteers from all over the country who are willing to help out and staff the events." According to Drift

Association's beliefs, everyone who spends time helping will somehow get something back in return from Drift Association. While the first Drift Day event had only 150 spectators, just four years later, the attendance at some events has reached 900 people. No matter how many spectators, Naoki tries to limit the event to 60 drivers, to ensure that all drivers get ample practice time. When Drift Day first started, the registration spots filled up in four to five days, but in four years of growing Drift Day events, the registration list fills up in as quickly as six hours, with 10–20 people on the waiting list. Naoki explains further, "Drift Association is successful because it is a very community-based company. We will give free track time to the volunteers, but some of the volunteers just want to belong. These guys really believe in drifting, and they want to do their part in helping to grow the sport. That right there is the key."

Japanese drifting magazines, such as Drift Tengoku (shown) and Battle Magazine, were instrumental in influencing the new audience of drifting enthusiasts in the United States. Since the new American drifting fans didn't have an English publication to read on the topic of drifting, it was only natural that they look at Japanese magazines, even if they couldn't necessarily understand what was written in Japanese kanji.

Pluspy videotape really inspired a lot of automotive enthusiasts and showed people how cool and exciting drifting could be. In fact, many of today's professional D1 drivers began drifting because they were inspired by this legendary video.

THE FIRST DRIFTING COMPETITIONS AND TEAMS

By the mid 1980s, it was common for small groups of drifting enthusiasts to practice their skills in the industrial areas, mountain passes (*touge*), and dock-side bay areas (*futou*) of Japan. However, in 1986, the Japanese magazine *Carboy* hosted its first drifting competition at an actual racetrack. That same year, *Carboy*'s competitor, *Video Option*, held a drifting contest called the Video Option Ikaten. This first Ikaten was more of a drifting showcase for the video shoot than an actual competition. The Ikaten was put together for groups of five cars to drift as a team. When grassroots drifters heard about the

Ikaten, drifters from all over Japan banded together to form teams to enter the popular event. Back then, some of the most famous and respected drift teams in Japan included teams such as Rough World, Running Free, ICBM, Drift Ensemble, K-Style, After-Fire, Rapid, FNR, Tinker, Night Zone, Response Family Sessions, Marionette, Break, Noisemaker, and Fluke. These teams are now legendary in Japan, and their individual members have greatly influenced the Japanese drifting industry as a whole.

THE EVOLUTION OF DRIFTING IN THE UNITED STATES

The art of drifting has been very popular with the hashiriya (street racers) in Japan since the late 1980s, but only since 2003 has it attracted mainstream media attention in the United States. With the ever-growing popularity of Japanese cars and JDM (Japanese domestic market) tuning parts in the United States, the art of drifting has rapidly become one of the most popular motorsports activities among Japanese and U.S. automotive enthusiasts alike.

Drifting became especially popular in California, as more and more motorsports enthusiasts began building cars for drifting instead of drag racing, and flocks of automotive enthusiasts from their late teens to mid-thirties turned their attention toward attending both amateur and professional drifting events instead of the traditional motorsports of autocross, drag, and roadracing.

INFLUENCE FROM JAPAN

Before there was a professional drifting series in the United States, underground groups of hardcore driving enthusiasts were already into drifting. Drifting culture in the United States didn't exactly happen overnight. As early as the late 1980s to mid-1990s, small groups of car enthusiasts from the United States discovered that they could find car magazines and racing videos at local Japanese bookstores and markets, like Kinokuniya or Asahiya bookstores.

These magazines and videos featured fixed-up cars that looked a lot different from the cars in the United States. Magazines like *Carboy*, *J's Tipo*, *Option*, *Option2*, *Revspeed*, *YoungVersion*, and *Autoworks* featured drifting cars, VIP-style cars

(high-end luxury sedan dress-up style), *bosozoku*-style cars (radical street gangster style), and full race cars like those of the Group A series, which eventually evolved into what we now know as Japan Grand Touring Championship (JGTC), or Super GT, racing. For these underground drifting enthusiasts, the car magazines and racing videos found at Japanese bookstores were amazing—it was like watching automotive porn. The magazines and videos provided inspiration to build cars different from what were popular in the United States at the time, and enjoy motorsports that were very different from the import drag racing scene that was exploding in the United States in the 1990s. Japanese media outlets showed a glimpse into the underground world of canyon racing and street drifting long before a professional series like D1 ever existed.

DRIFT CAR THEORY

For many of the people who discovered Japanese media outlets during the early stages of drifting in the United States, the magazines and videos they saw influenced the types of cars they built. The underground street racing styles from Japan were the complete opposite of the horrific, painted-vinyl interiors, knock-off Supra wings, "Powered by Honda" stickers, and side-marker lights that plagued the cars of the U.S. import car scene. Instead of building Civics, Accords, Eclipses, Preludes, and Integras for street drag racing, the drifting trendsetters built cars to be driven at their limits in SCCA and NASA autocross and road-racing events, and to attack the winding roads of their local mountain or canyon. Front engine, rear-wheel-drive (FR) cars like the Nissan 240SX (S13, S14), Toyota Corolla (AE86), Mazda RX7 (SA22C, FA, FB, FC3S), Nissan 300Z (Z32), and Toyota Supra (MA60, MA70, JZA80) were some of the more popular cars for early U.S. drifters. The people who had been exposed to this very different Japanese car culture were completely ahead of their time; they were the real trendsetters of the JDM scene long before the controversial term "JDM" was ever coined.

BUILDING THE DRIVER

With the newfound exposure to drifting and functionally modified cars, underground driving enthusiasts began to change their way of thinking. They modified their cars for function, as well as form. The early drifters emphasized suspension tuning, good tires, and brake upgrades before making engine modifications. They made their cars faster by first learning how to *drive* faster, mastering traditional grip-driving first—braking in a straight line before the corner, accelerating out of the apex of the turn, practicing heel-and-toe braking.

Early drifting enthusiasts attended sanctioned autocross events to practice maneuvering their cars through tight, technical turns. As their skills increased, many drivers began going to roadracing events to feel what it's like to control a car at higher speeds.

Autocross and road-racing events were good for letting the drivers test their cars' suspensions, but a lot of these drivers wanted more. With the constant influence of Japanese drifting magazines and videos, underground drivers wanted to drift. There was only one problem: strict SCCA organizers were furious when drivers attempted drifting on the autocross courses! Drifters often attempted to get sideways and ended up knocking over cones that the volunteer SCCA course workers worked so hard to set up. Furthermore, nervous SCCA officials scolded drivers who tried to drift at autocross events, saying that drifters were continually endangering the safety of course workers by sliding around turns, or— even worse—spinning out. It just wasn't working out; drifting was not welcome at autocross events.

THE BEGINNING OF SPEEDTRIAL USA DRIFTING

On January 30, 2000, SpeedTrial USA held the very first roadracing event of its kind at Buttonwillow Raceway Park, California, specifically inviting drifters to practice drifting at the circuit. At this first on-track drifting event, Tommy Chen from SpeedTrial split the raceway into two courses: the West Loop was for roadracing only, the East Loop was opened up for drifting practice, but it also allowed road racers to drive laps while waiting for their next run group on the West Loop. Early drifters including Mark Hutchinson and Dave Scholz from Slide Squad, Alex Villareal, Benson Hsu, Herb Policarpio, and Richard Tang attended, along with hardcore drifting fanatics, like Alex Pfeiffer and Battle Swing, his team from the

The First Time U.S. Organizers Brought Pro Japanese Drifters to SoCal

An early milestone for drifting in the United States was Sunday, February 24, 2002: the first event arranged by U.S. promoters in which professional drifters were flown in from Japan to do a drifting demo on the U.S. mainland.

Thanks to Tommy Chen from SpeedTrial USA, Moto Miwa from Club4AG, and Jon Kaneda from JIC USA, drifting enthusiasts in California were able to spend a day at Buttonwillow Raceway driving and hanging out with Hiroshi Takahashi from the legendary AE86 drift team "Running Free" from the Kanagawa area, and Shinji Minowa from "Hey Man!" a team of AE86 drivers from the Yokota area that formed Japan's first drift team with American members. Takahashi and Minowa drifted around Buttonwillow's East Course using Tommy Chen's white S13 240SX and Moto Miwa's red AE86 coupe. The scene was very small and grassroots at the time; there were no huge banners, flags, Jumbotron TV screens—just plenty of cars lined up in the pits with jacks, toolboxes, ice chests with drinks, and of course, lots of extra wheels and tires.

California teams and drivers in attendance included Alex Pfeiffer, Taka Aono, Charlie Ongsingco, Bryan Norris, Benson Hsu, Terry Henderson, Al Lagura, Kenta Ogawara, and many members of Club4AG, Battle Swing, and Cipher Garage, and Slide Squad.

San Francisco Bay Area. Pfeiffer and Battle Swing caravanned down from the Bay Area in their AE86s, driving their drift cars for five hours or more just to practice drifting without getting hassled. This was the very beginning of the SpeedTrial USA Drifting program, and for the Bay Area drivers, the five-hour commute was definitely worth it.

The SpeedTrial USA drifting events were the beginning of a revolution, as more and more drivers began taking their drifting off the streets and onto the track, shifting the focus to a safer drifting environment. However, as time went by, a rift began between the grip drivers (road racers) and the drifters. Grip drivers complained that the drift group was constantly running off the track, kicking up dirt or other debris onto the track. Drifters got a bad rep among traditional road racers, and every time a grip driver spun out as a result of excess dirt on the racetrack, guess who was to blame? That's right, the drifters.

But, the grip drivers weren't the only ones complaining. The drifters experienced frustration as well, saying that there sometimes was not enough time allocated for the drift groups to practice. There were also instances of grip drivers tailgating the drifters, trying to pass and pressuring the drifters to

drive at speeds higher than what they were comfortable with—not necessarily a nurturing environment for novice drifters to hone their skills. To top it off, many racetrack managers complained that the drifters were "tearing up the racetrack with their skidding tires." This was not always true—the rapidly spinning street tires from the rear of a drift car at speed actually put less stress on the pavement than the slick, grippy race tires on a roadracing car—but racetrack owners had made up their minds. Once again, the drifters needed a place where they could just go and drift.

The early drifting events promoted by SpeedTrial USA and Club4AG were instrumental in the growth of the U.S. drifting culture. However, drifters slowly trickled out of that environment, seeking a safe, dedicated atmosphere where they could practice *drifting only*, without pressure of tailgating and without old-fashioned track officials screaming about the cars "getting too squirrelly out there." The popularity and head count of the early drifting practice events eventually led to the formation of new drifting-only event organizers like Drift Association on the West Coast, DGTrials on the East Coast, and Drift Session in Hawaii.

Mainstream Productions and Drift Session Bring Signal Auto to Hawaii

Not long after Speedtrial USA and Club4AG held the first Japanese drifting demo by a U.S. organizer on the mainland, things were in motion to bring Japanese drifters to Hawaii. Mainstream Productions founder Ken Miyoshi and his brother Shige were transporting the Signal Auto S13 "strawberry face" Sileighty around the continental United States and Canada for Import Showoff car shows and made plans to bring the car to Hawaii for its annual Streetcar Showoff in Honolulu. When Dave Shimokawa from Drift Session heard about the possibility of the Signal Sileighty coming to Hawaii, he contacted Ken to work out a deal. Dave wanted Ken to keep the car in Hawaii for a week after the big car show so Signal Auto could do a drifting demo for Hawaii's amateur drifters. Drift Session was already holding local events at Hawaii Raceway Park, but at this time, the Hawaiian drivers had not yet seen a drifting demonstration by high-level Japanese drivers.

After the two came to terms, Mainstream Productions partnered with Drift Session to organize the first-ever drifting demo by a Japanese driver in Hawaii on September 1, 2002. Drift Session flew in Signal's driver, Fumiaki Komatsu from Signal Auto in Osaka, Japan, to do the demonstration. While Drift

Session was holding regular events at the raceway park, this was Ken Miyoshi's first experience in putting together a drifting event. It was a momentous event for Hawaiian drivers, as it gave them a frame of reference for improving their drifting skills. Photos of the event appeared in major U.S. magazines as well as small magazines, such as *LA AutoGuide*. Hawaii's own Grip Video released footage from the event in Volume 2 of their Grip Video series. The event was even featured in Japan's well-known *Battle Magazine*.

(S13 and S14) and the Toyota Corolla GT-S (AE86). More events, such as the Falken Drift Showoff by Mainstream Productions and RS-R Drift Festival, added fuel to the fire as drifting started making its way into the mainstream.

By mid-2003, the excitement of drifting in the mainstream media had blown up faster than grassroots drifters had expected, or even wanted. Magazines began featuring "drift cars" or writing articles about "how to build a drift car" to keep up with competition, as hordes of uninvolved journalists wrote less-than-accurate reports of what this new drifting phenomenon was all about. However, many of the real grassroots drifting enthusiasts had a hard time relating to these types of mainstream media outlets, many of which failed to report about what grassroots drifters felt was the first step in putting together a drift car: building up the driver's skills.

By June 2003, everyone was talking about Slipstream Global Marketing bringing Japan's professional drift series, the D1 Grand Prix, to the United States. The D1 Driver Search qualifying rounds were held at Irwindale Speedway, and the top 40 U.S. drifters were judged by some of the top drifting experts in Japan, including Keiichi Tsuchiya, Manabu Suzuki, Dai Inada, and Manabu Orido. In the end, only eight U.S. drivers qualified for the D1: Calvin Wan, Ken Gushi, Bryan Norris, Hubert Young, Rich Rutherford, Ernie Fixmer, Sam Hubinette, and Daijiro Yoshihara. This elite group of eight drivers battled with the top-ranked drifters of Japan at the first official D1 event in the United States on August 31, 2003.

At the August D1 event, everyone was excited to see how well the new U.S. drifters would fare against the seasoned pro drifters of Japan. The U.S. drivers definitely put up a good fight, but nevertheless, they could not match the experience and driving skill of the legendary Japanese drivers, who took all three podium positions.

November 2003, brought a groundbreaking announcement from Slipstream Productions at the SEMA Tradeshow in Las Vegas. In a small conference room filled with top drivers, sponsors, and media members from the United States and Japan, Slipstream announced it would create a new drifting series in North America: Formula Drift.

ENTER DRIFT DAY

One of the best-known drifting event organizers is Drift Association, an organization that runs the Drift Day events on the West Coast. The events are slightly similar to an autocross, but allow drivers to practice drifting around cones in a safe, controlled environment (usually a wide-open parking lot) with tutorials by seasoned drifters. Some of the earliest Drift Day instructors include Taka Aono, Hiro Sumida, Kenji Sakai, Alex Pfeiffer, Andy Yen, Calvin Wan, and Ken Gushi. At these events, novice drifters practice drifting techniques and get used to the equilibrium of a sideways-moving car. The focus of Drift Days was

to take drifting *off the streets* so the emerging drifting scene would not attract negative attention from law enforcement and media as the street drag races did. With this safe, sanctioned environment, people improved their skills rapidly and dramatically, learning how to drift longer, faster, and at more extreme angles. As grassroots U.S. drivers improved their skills, the sport's popularity grew.

Talk of this new and exciting underground form of racing spread among the JDM import crowd of Southern California, as new would-be drifters sold their Civics and Integras in favor of popular FR platform cars like the Nissan 240SX

Video Option USA Ikaten Irwindale Speedway, January 17, 2003

On January 17, 2003, the producers of Option flew in from Japan to shoot "Video Option Ikaten (drift contest)" at Irwindale Speedway, California. Amateur U.S. drifters were invited to compete in a grassroots drift competition held in the parking lot of Irwindale Speedway. Many amateur drifters in California entered the event, as this was their first chance to be seen and recognized by the famous Japanese video crew. Even then, the event was not widely publicized in the automotive aftermarket industry, and the general car show–going public didn't know it was going to happen. Japanese celebrity drivers Akira Iida, Tarzan Yamada, Ken Nomura, and Daijiro Inada were on hand to judge the event. The course was laid out in the parking lot with cones and was held at night. Option taped each run, and the winners of the event received small prizes, not to mention the respect of their peers. This was the first event to bring major media attention to the drifters in the United States. Even though they were still at a novice level compared with most Japanese drifters, the seed had been planted.

The first-place winner was Andy Yen, driving a cream-colored spray-painted 1985 AE86 Corolla GT-S coupe. Second place went to Javier Paramo, driving a 1983 MA60 Toyota Supra, powered by a twin turbocharged 2JZGTE engine out of a 1998 Supra. Third place was awarded to Alex Pfeiffer, who had just recently purchased his now-famous turbocharged 1985 AE86 Corolla GT-S (it was silver at the time) from Stan Lee.

When the North American drivers assembled at Road Atlanta in April 2004 for the inaugural Formula Drift event, most of them were novice drifters—even though many of the sponsors and media had been hyping them as American "pro drifters." Whether or not all the hype surrounding them was true, these young drivers were, in fact, the top drifters in the United States—and they had to grow into their pro racing shoes rather quickly. Of the competitors in Atlanta, there was a small handful of drivers present with professional racing or rally experience—Rhys Millen, Samuel Hubinette, Ryan Hampton—however, most of the other drivers had very little racing experience. Some of them had never done anything on a racetrack but drift.

The U.S. drivers grew a lot in the inaugural year of Formula Drift, many of them starting the season as novice drivers and ending the season as professional drifters. They had been on a tour across America, driving in competitions and spreading the love and excitement of drifting by performing demonstrations in front of audiences that had not previously seen drifting; shredding across the pavement, transforming their tires into thick white clouds of smoke, spitting up smoldering chunks of rubber, and marking up the concrete every place they went. The kid gloves were off, and these once-novice drivers had become the new generation of drifting stars in the United States. In this first year of Formula D, the drivers had accomplished what the seasoned D1 drift veterans of Japan had not—they formed a connection with the younger "MTV" generation. With all the new sponsors and media attention the series received, coverage of Formula Drift began appearing in several magazines stateside and internationally, stirring up attention from overseas drivers, fans, and sponsors.

With bad-boy drivers like Alex Pfeiffer and Andy Yen, and rowdy teams like the infamous Drift Alliance, these drivers had become stars in their own right. Not to mention the seventeen-year-old drifting protégé and media darling Ken Gushi, who, by the end of the series, had a stronger fan base in the United States than some of the legendary D1 drivers that he himself looked up to.

To legitimize Formula D in North America, Slipstream enlisted the help of SCCA Pro Racing to sanction the four-event series. While Formula D was created as a North American drift series, entries were not limited to U.S. entrants. Also included in the 2004 series were invitational drifting demonstrations at traditional racing events—a Champ Car race at Laguna Seca, *Road & Track Magazine*'s International Drifting Shootout, and Falken Tire's Drifting Demo at the famed Pike's Peak International Hillclimb.

EXPOSURE TO DRIFTING:
Influential Magazines and Websites

Early Japanese Magazines with Drifting Content

Drift Tengoku   Option2
YoungVersion   Revspeed
Autoworks   Carboy

First Japanese Magazine Feature on Drifting in America

In the March 2001 issue of *Drift Tengoku* (*Drift Heaven*) *Magazine* a freelance writer named Kenta Ogawara wrote the first feature on U.S. drifters ever published in a Japanese car magazine. This was a big deal for drifting in the United States, because it announced to Japan that there were actually people in America following in the footsteps of the legendary drift teams of Japan, who commonly practiced drifting at *touge* (mountain) or *futou* (bayside) areas, based on their geographic location. Drift teams battled each other, attacking the mountain roads to perfect their driving. *Drift Tengoku Magazine*, or "Dori-Ten," as it is commonly called in Japan, is an offshoot and subsidiary of Option, Japan's largest and most powerful publisher of automotive performance magazines. Almost all of Japan's drifters read *Dori-Ten*, and Ogawara's two-page spread on drifting in America was one of the issue's main feature stories.

The issue featured a photo spread of Andy Yen drifting his red 1985 Corolla GT-S coupe on one of Southern California's mountain roads. Even though the Corolla was underpowered compared with the other cars on the mountain, Andy was one of Southern California's fastest canyon drivers. The article showed the location of the mountain area, as well as some small photos of Yen's AE86 and Benson Hsu's black S13 Sileighty as they practiced drifting in remote industrial areas. It also featured a small sidebar, explaining to Japanese readers the differences between the Japanese market S13 Silvia/180SX and the U.S. market 240SX, and between the Japanese market AE86 Levin/Trueno and the U.S. market AE86 Corolla GT-S.

Early U.S. Magazines with Drifting Content

SuperStreet	*Automobile*
Grassroots Motorsports	*Modified*
Access Unlimited Magazine	*Car & Driver*

HASHIRIYA BATTLE MAGAZINE

Battle Magazine (usually referred to as *BM*) was legendary in Japan for being the most influential magazine for grassroots-level drifting in Japan. *BM*'s parent company, a small publisher called Heiwa Publishing, printed the first issue in 1990, and intitally called the magazine *Hashiriya Battle Magazine*, focusing its content on both motorcycles and drift cars. In 1996, the magazine switched its content to drifting cars only.

Battle Magazine focused mostly on real street cars and amateur drifting teams, and had a small section that profiled scale-model cars that people modified to look like drifting cars. There were even photos of people

drifting on bicycles! *BM* was willing to print photos of drift cars actually owned by amateur drivers, with beat-up aero kits, zipties, or even missing bumpers. *BM* also featured profiles of smaller drifting shops and street drift teams, so even though it was a smaller magazine, almost everyone looked at *BM* regularly. This created a stronger reader connection than that of Dori-Ten. *BM*'s readers felt that the magazine really cared about the street scene, and as a result, a ton of the grassroots drifters bought *BM* on a monthly basis.

Battle Magazine hosted a drifting competition series for amateurs, the BM Cup, but in Japan, everyone referred to it as "BM Hi." Even though the competition was created for amateur drifters, the caliber of the unsponsored drivers and privately owned personal cars in the BM Cup Series was extremely high, even higher than that of most drivers in the U.S. Formula D series in 2005. *Battle Magazine* started the BM Cup in 1997, with competitions at

Nikko Circuit and the legendary Ebisu Circuit. BM Cup was a points series, and the drivers competed not only for individual podium wins, but for total points throughout the year. The first series champion of the BM Cup Series was Ken Maeda from a drift team called DP2 in Kanagawa. Maeda went on to drive the yellow Up Garage AE86 in the D1 Grand Prix series. The close runner-up was Fukuda of the renowned drift team Fluke, who also went on to compete in D1 with his yellow RPS13 180SX. *BM* featured photos from these events and sometimes included a free DVD with event footage in the magazine's frequent "reader's presents," which were usually limited-edition stickers packaged with the magazine.

In the United States, *BM* was influential because it showed what real Japanese "street drifting" style looked like. The cars had a different look to them— more raw and hard core. There weren't many sponsor stickers on the cars, only stickers of their own teams or teams they respected. If there were shop stickers on a car, it was usually because that's where the car got built, or the driver was a friend of the shop.

BM showcased different kinds of cars, from *boro* (beat up) drift machines to full carshow-level drift cars. There were features on different styles of cars, including old-school style S13s and A31 Cefiros with deep-dish 15 inch wheels and *oni-kyan*, or demon camber. A demon camber car had ridiculous amounts of negative camber up front, and negative roll center adjusters, or longer control arms so that the bottom of the wheels actually stuck out from the fenders, instead of just adjusting camber with your typical camber plates on top of the strut tower. Back in the day, it was also very popular to spray paint the car's wheels black, to use zipties on the fenders, and to attach front lip spoilers. *BM* provided a way for American viewers to soak in all the style and culture behind drifting in Japan, something most magazines (especially U.S. drifting magazines) never featured.

It was very difficult to find *Battle Magazine* at Japanese bookstores in the United States. In Los Angeles, only the most ambitious of magazine readers could get *BM*.

In 2001, *Battle Magazine* became the first Japanese magazine to regularly report on the U.S.

Demon Camber

For true demon camber style, the car must not only have negative camber, but the wheels must be pushed out on the bottom, so that they stick out from the fenders and bumpers like crazy. If an AE86 owner wanted to emulate the Rough World–style demon camber, they would need to use adjustable camber plates on top, as well as longer control arms or negative roll center adjusters to widen the front track of the car. Also, of course, the wheels must be super wide with stretched tires to complete the look. If the wheels aren't wide, the visual effect of demon camber is lessened. Again, demon camber is not based on functional amounts of negative camber, but on *ridiculous* amounts of camber.

drifting scene, through a monthly column called "Outer Drifter's Style" by Kenta Ogawara, who was nicknamed "Kentax" in the magazine. This well-read column reported on drifting as it emerged and flourished in the United States, featuring drifting events in Hawaii and Southern California. The editor of *Battle Magazine*, Shinichi Takahashi, really cared about drifting, and was willing to give drifting columnists from the United States a chance. The magazine ran features on up-and-coming drifters from California like Calvin Wan, Ken Gushi, Andy Yen, Javier Paramo, Ernie Fixmer, and others. Frequent reports on drifting, and talk of bigger events such as D1 USA, drift demos at the annual SEMA Show in Las Vegas, and Formula Drift in the United States, piqued the interest of the column's regular readers, who included not just amateur drivers, but also notable Japanese drifting stars like Nobushige Kumakubo, Kazuhiro Tanaka, Nobuteru Taniguchi, and Ken Maeda.

At the end of 2005, Japan's legendary and influential *Battle Magazine* closed its doors due to financial problems with its parent publishing company, but its fan base still lives on. For those who sought out the raw footage of real drifting culture in Japan through

Battle Magazine month after month, the magazine truly did its part to keep the pure spirit of drifting alive. *BM* is sorely missed.

GRASSROOTS MOTORSPORTS MAGAZINE

Grassroots Motorsports is a traditional American motorsports magazine, focusing mostly on autocross and roadracing, with lots of informative car buildup stories and tech articles.

David S. Wallens, *GRM*'s well-respected editor-in-chief, was open minded enough to give drifting a chance, and ran drifting photos of icon AE86 driver Katsuhiro Ueo winning first place at the first-ever D1 Grand Prix in the United States in the December 2003 issue. A feature article about the 240SX also showcased a photo of Ken Gushi's first car, a champagne metallic S13 240SX.

In February 2004, *GRM* followed up on their previous issue and shocked many of their readers by running a cover story on drifting. At the time, a large feature like this was a big deal for the drifting world, since many early drifting enthusiasts were also active at autocross events, and almost everyone read and relied on *Grassroots Motorsports* as a top source of information. The February 2004 issue— featuring a drifting photo of Calvin Wan's red FD3S RX7 on the cover—had a ten-page drifting feature, which *GRM* referred to as "the biggest automotive sensation since the Drive-In." The cover story told readers how to get involved in drifting on a grassroots level, and explained basic drifting techniques and car setup. The feature also included interviews with representatives from Falken Tire Corporation, Yokohama Tire Corporation, SCCA Pro Racing, US Drift by NASA (National Auto Sport Association), and a driver profile on up-and-coming driver Calvin Wan.

This particular issue of *GRM* caused quite a stir among its readership. As letters poured into the

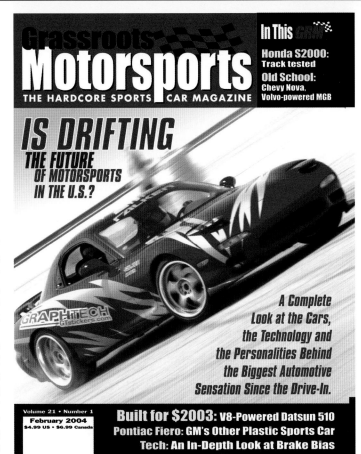

editorial offices, the *GRM* website's message boards lit up with debates on whether or not the readers were for or against drifting. Some argued that drifting was not a valid motorsport since it was not timed, but others were more open minded, fully supporting drifting as a valid motorsport and something the magazine should continue to cover.

What ever the case may be, the controversial *Grassroots Motorsports* drifting issue woke up the conservative readership of the magazine and caused them to take notice of drifting as a growing motorsport phenomenon. Interestingly enough, *GRM* later reported that their drifting issue was one of their magazine's top-selling issues at the newsstands.

CarCulture in *LA AutoGuide*

LA AutoGuide was a free biweekly magazine distributed widely at automotive shops, bookstores, Japanese markets, cafés, and restaurants in Southern California, all the way from the Los Angeles area to San Diego. It had all sorts of ads from local performance shops and JDM parts importers.

The thing that set *LA AutoGuide* apart from the other typical Japanese free magazines was its content, which had a different style than most magazines because of the drifting photos it contained, the language it was written in (slang terminology for young people), and the subject matter it covered.

Due to its "CarCulture" column, *LA AutoGuide* became the first U.S. magazine focused on the emerging drifting scene in the United States. Every two weeks, "CarCulture" provided regular reports on drifting events, from *real hardcore drifting enthusiasts* with real drifting content—something no other American magazine covered, or even knew about. On top of that, the magazine was free! "CarCulture" featured real-deal drift cars that people saw on the street or at events—ghetto ziptied and spray painted cars with a single racing seat and bashed-in fenders. Of course, it ran photos of pro drivers and their clean professional-looking cars, too, but it was really the underground "street" drifting culture that was close to enthusiasts' hearts. "CarCulture" covered things such as local Drift Day events, D1 Grand Prix, Formula Drift events around the country, Drift Showoff events, JGTC, and even photos from Japan,

such as the BigX Drifting Festival at Ebisu Circuit, VIP style and drift cars at Tokyo Auto Salon, and other private drift events in Japan.

With the success of the "CarCulture" column, *LA AutoGuide* began to increase in popularity among the import community in Southern California, and more and more advertisers began jumping on board. People from around the country were reading *LA AutoGuide*, and were constantly in search of issues.

With columns that focused almost completely on drifting, with contributions from top drifting experts from the United States and Japan, *LA AutoGuide* was completely ahead of its time. Unfortunately, the publisher had a falling out with his partner in the magazine, and all the contributions of drifting content suddenly stopped as well, leaving a void in Southern California's drifting community.

Early American Websites with Drifting Content (in English)

Club4AG	www.club4ag.com
Slide Squad	www.davescholz.com
Team Cipher	www.ciphergarage.com
Battle Version	www.battleversion.com
Drift Club	www.driftclub.com
Drift Session	www.driftsession.com
Kaz's AE86 Project	(no longer available)
CTA Ken Driftmania	(no longer available)

Drift Club
www.driftclub.com

Bryan Norris put together the Drift Club website at the end of 1999. He got the name from the Drift Club video series, which was the first all-drifting video that Sunpros (Video Option) ever made. It was a small, short-lived series, with fewer than 10 tapes, but it was one of Bryan's favorite videos. He originally put the website up because he was new to the Internet, and wanted to create a website with drifting content, so he bought a scanner, and scanned in photos that he took, as well as pages out of magazines he liked.

As a driver, Bryan understood the mechanics of drifting, but contacted Moto Miwa for some help on translating and writing the Drift Club website's section on drifting techniques.

Bryan also had a thing for Nissan Skylines. He asked Tsuyoshi Inoue at 5Zigen USA to help him translate and write the history of the Skyline. Bryan also included the history of Keiichi Tsuchiya, using information he got from Japanese books or videos.

After he added a message board to the site, many Southern Californians who ran touge posted messages with the dates and times where they would run or the spots where they should meet up before making the ascent up the mountain. However, after a while, Bryan's busy schedule at work caught up with him, and he no longer had time to maintain or update the site. The site is still up, but he hasn't really had the time to keep the content current.

Team Cipher (Cipher Garage)
www.ciphergarage.com

In 1995 or 1996, I began to put together the "Team Cipher" website, named after our car crew (now called Cipher Garage). The site featured pictures of all our cars, which were mostly AE86s and other old-school Toyotas, as well as short articles and captioned photos I took at autocross events and import car shows.

As far as I know, the Team Cipher website was one of the first U.S. websites to feature information and content about AE86s, Japanese car culture, and drifting. It was written casually, with an abundance of American and Filipino slang terms, sarcasm, and terminology dealing with Japanese cars. Even though it originally started out as a site dedicated to old-school Toyotas, it rapidly evolved once I got deeper and deeper into Japanese drifting culture. When I went to Japan in 1999 for the first time, I posted a full event report over several pages, with photos of drift cars, wangan cars, and even some early VIP cars.

When I moved to Southern California in 1999, I was faced with a dilemma. There were just so many car-related events happening on a regular basis in the Los Angeles area, you could easily go to an event once

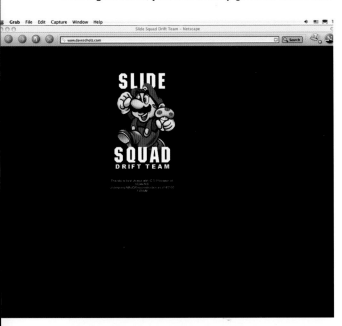

Slide Squad's early website.

or twice a week! I could either stay at home and work on the website, or go out and live the 86 life with all my new AE86 friends. Needless to say, progress on the website kind of stopped there, but there are definite plans to bring it back!

Club4AG
www.club4ag.com

Officially established by Moto Miwa in November 1997, Club4AG is one of the best and most well-known Internet resources for drifting and cars with 4AG engines. It was first started as an informational website, keeping track of things that Moto experienced in building his AE86 Corolla Levin, but it was expanded to host reference material for other people building cars. Eventually a message board was added to get opinions and feedback from other 4AG owners, and it evolved into a huge public forum that had posts from Corolla owners all over the world. Through the member-based forums and tech articles on Club4AG, Moto educated a lot of people on the Internet, and taught them not just about Corollas, but also about drifting.

When early stars in drifting, such as Alex Pfeiffer, started posting information about drifting on the forums, even more people became interested in the site. It introduced drifting to people who didn't even know what it was. Back then, Moto captured small MPEG files from his collection of Best Motoring videos, and posted them on the site. Best Motoring International eventually

contacted him and asked him to take the videos down, but for most people who didn't live in California or didn't have access to Japanese videos, this was the first time they saw drifting.

As the website grew in hits and forum members, it promoted grassroots track-day functions, like SpeedTrial USA, roadracing, and drifting events. As word of these events spread, more non-Corolla owners signed up for the website's forums as well, just to get information on the drifting events. These events, which were staffed by hard-working volunteer members of the Club4AG Website, later became known as Drift Day.

Early Videos
Japanese videotapes with drifting footage were instrumental to the growth of the U.S. drifting movement. Option and Option2 videos were the first glimpses into the drifting world for people in the United States, since the Option series was the most widely known and had the best distribution, even though Japanese car videotapes were still difficult to find.

Early on, the best places to find Japanese videos for sale were Japanese bookstores. J-Wave Video in Little Tokyo's Japanese Village Plaza was a cool store. It was easy to get a membership card at J-Wave, and they rented Japanese car videos! We rented the videos and set up another VCR to dub them as we watched them. I remember one of the first videos I rented was an original VHS copy of the

Carboy DoriCon GP, *Drift Tengoku* video, and we found a tape that was actually a movie, not a "car video" like the Option series. There were five movies in the series, which was called Shutokou Trial, after the highway in Tokyo. It featured some *wangan* (highway) racing and drifting. In some of the videos, Keiichi Tsuchiya made cameo appearances, and in the last video, *Trial 5: The Final Battle*, the star of the movie had to drift against Keiichi. This movie was incredibly cool because it had an actual storyline. It was made long before American movies like *The Fast & the Furious*, so you can imagine how disappointed we were when the first Fast & Furious film came out, with less-than-accurate depictions of import street racing and such. In our endless search for cool Japanese car videos, there were few videos that really stood out. Those that did included the following:

Best Motoring, Volume 41 and Volume 42

In late 1998 and early 1999, Best Motoring Video released their groundbreaking Volumes 41 and 42, featuring the Drift King, Keiichi Tsuchiya, and his white 1986 AE86 Sprinter Trueno GTV, which was fully built up by TRD Japan. The video featured Japanese drifting stars like Keiichi Tsuchiya, Nobuteru Taniguchi, Nobushige Kumakubo, Manabu Orido, Akira Iida, and others demonstrating drifting with white AE86s at the "Holy Land of Drifting," Ebisu Circuit's Minami (South) Course. I got the next tape in the series, Volume 42, featured Keiichi driving his newly built TRD Works AE86 Levin hatchback with N2 flares and super-wide RS Watanabe wheels. It also had a drifting instructional segment from Ebisu Circuit, where Keiichi, Kumakubo, Taniguchi, Orido, and the others taught and demonstrated drifting in their white AE86s.

Pluspy Video

In 2001, I met Osamu Ishida, a manager from Advan in Japan, at SEMA. He knew I was an AE86 maniac, so he brought me some AE86 magazines and a dubbed videotape. The tape was a very old racing video with Keiichi Tsuchiya in his old car, which turned out to be the legendary Pluspy video! This was the first drifting video, and it featured Keiichi drifting on the mountain roads of Japan in his mildly street tuned AE86. It was nothing like the D1 level drifting that we're all used to seeing nowadays, but this was the first video that Keiichi did, and it made him famous and inspired incredible amounts of Japanese street racers to get into drifting.

Initial D

The topic of the *Initial D* comic and anime series is subject to a lot of debate in the drifting community. *Initial D* was first drawn as a Japanese comic book, but it became so popular, that an anime (cartoon) series was eventually planned. When the anime first came out, it became wildly popular, especially in Japan, Hong Kong, and Taiwan. The video series aired on Japanese television in the late 1990s. The story of *Initial D* was based on underground street racing, drifting, and touge, but also included comedy and a love story. The drawings and representation of the cars were so realistic, all the way down to the how the cars sounded, moved, and even minor details like the lights on the gauge clusters. The characters in *Initial D* drove realistic cars that were popular with the hashiriya in Japan—FC3S RX7, FD3S RX7, S13 Silvia, S13 Sileighty, EG6 Civic, and AE86 Levin and Trueno. The realism of the cars and the story really contributed to the success of *Initial D*.

The young star of the show, Takumi Fujiwara, drove a panda (black-and-white) 1985 AE86 Sprinter Trueno GT-Apex to deliver tofu for his dad in the early morning before he went to school and to his part-time job at the gas station. Takumi had to drive through "Mount Akina" (using a mountain road based on the touge in the Gunma region of Japan) while on deliveries and he had to practice the smoothness of his driving lines so he wouldn't break the tofu in the trunk of the car. In the cartoon series, Takumi encountered many touge drivers who wanted to race him on the mountain.

On web forums, such as Club4AG, some drifters and AE86 owners complained that the *Initial D* cartoon attracted too many posers to the scene, brought inexperienced kids to crash their cars in the canyons, and drove up the prices of AE86 hatchbacks. In some way, there was truth behind their complaints, as the huge success and popularity of *Initial D* got really out of hand in Southern California at one point. Whatever the case may be, *Initial D* publicized AE86s, touge running, and drifting, whether people think it to be a good thing or a bad thing. *Initial D*'s success brought new people to the drifting scene, as well as new business in the form of merchandising, including *Initial D* die-cast cars, radio-control cars, video games, adaptations of the comic book and cartoon series in English, arcade games, posters, stuffed animals, and more. *Initial D* had a huge and lasting impact in the world of drifting.

Drift Club

Drift Club was a short-lived video series made by Sunpros, also known as Video Option. It was one of the first videos that Sunpros ever made that featured just drifting. The first *Drift Club* video was a "How To Drift" video. It featured Keiichi Tsuchiya, of course, and an all-star cast of famous Japanese drifters when they were still young.

EARLY DRIFTING EVENTS

This 1983 MA60 Toyota Supra was nicknamed the JZA60 because early drifter Javier Paramo removed the original 5MGE engine and swapped in a 2JZGTE engine from a 1998 Supra Turbo. With all the horsepower and torque in this Supra, Javier loved to drift using power oversteer, even though he learned to drift with other techniques in a low-horsepower Corolla. Taken on the morning of the first RS-R Drift Festival at Irwindale, this photo shows the Supra sitting on 16x10 (front) and 16x11 (rear) negative offset 3piece Epsilon wheels.

RS-R DRIFT FESTIVAL
April 6, 2003, Irwindale Speedway,
Irwindale, California

First place at the RS-R Drift Festival was awarded to Alex Pfeiffer, with second-place going to Alex's future teammate Andy Yen, and Craig Fisher receiving third place. Little did Alex know that this was only the start of his relationship with RS-R, as he would become the driver of the RS-R turbocharged Honda S2000 used in the Formula D series.

Tsukasa Gushi, owner of Gushi Auto, was one of the first drifting supporters in Southern California. At his old shop in San Gabriel, California, Gushi built and serviced most of the AE86 Corollas and 240SXs that were involved in the early years of So-Cal drifting. Gushi Auto was the preferred maintenance and repair shop for AE86 Corolla owners; because Gushi and every single one of his mechanics were AE86 owners themselves—and, Gushi himself was crazy about drifting. It was during early drifting sessions at El Mirage's desert lake bed that he taught his son Kenshiro how to drift. Back then, Gushi-san was just trying to teach his son about rally driving, but discovered that Ken was a natural born drifter. Gushi-san admits, "When Ken [started becoming] good, I thought it was so awesome. I'm so proud of him."

But even for himself, he continues, "Drifting [has become] a big part of my personality. Drifting is my life. Man, I can't stop drifting. But one thing, I hope the grassroots Drift Day–style events become more popular, not just Formula D all the time. I want more new people to get involved in drifting; if the grassroots events happen more, we can have more drifting drivers, not just drifting spectators. Just five years ago, we were all nobody . . . we would just go to Tommy's [Speed Thai USA] events at Buttonwillow and drift for fun. But nowadays only Drift Association

and Charlie [Just Drift] are mostly doing the small drifting events out here. Right now when you go to Formula D, all the main cars [cost] over two-hundred-thousand dollars. But I want to see more basic fun FR cars coming out to drift. It's easy to get involved, just bring your own car to the racetrack or parking lot events, and start from there. I think people shouldn't just watch drifting. Get involved yourself and start driving!" But even for himself, he continues, "Drifting [has become] a big part of my personality. Drifting is my life. Man, I can't stop drifting. But one thing, I hope the grassroots Drift Day–style events become more popular, not just Formula D all the time. I want more new people to get involved in drifting; if the grassroots events happen more, we can have more drifting drivers, not just drifting spectators. Just five years ago, we were all nobody . . . we would just go to Tommy's [Speed Thai USA] events at Buttonwillow and drift for fun. But nowadays only Drift Association and Charlie [Just Drift] are mostly doing the small drifting events out here. Right now when you go to Formula D, all the main cars [cost] over two-hundred-thousand dollars. But I want to see more basic fun FR cars coming out to drift. It's easy to get involved, just bring your own car to the racetrack or parking lot events, and start from there. I think people shouldn't just watch drifting. Get involved yourself and start driving!"

DRIFT DAY 5

May 25, 2003.
Irwindale Speedway Parking Lot,
Irwindale, California

Kenshiro Gushi practicing at Irwindale with his newly put together S13 coupe. The car had factory champagne metallic paint, a light brown interior with a Nardi Classic steering wheel, SR20DET engine, and RS Watanabe RS8 three-piece wheels.

(1) Mike Urbano was out practicing in his brother Brian's 1986 AE86 coupe, one of the first in California with a 20v 4AGE engine. Brian's "Black Limited" version coupe AE86 had OEM Japanese kouki bumpers front and back, with the rare "Black LTD" edition gold Trueno emblem, Saft towhook from Cipher Garage's own HerbrockOne, zenki front lip spoiler, OEM JDM rear spoiler, and Toysport copy side skirts. He changed the OEM clear "corner bumper lenses" for amber lenses from the Japanese version AE86 SR. Wrapped in Yokohama ES100 tires, the wheels up front are 14x8 (+0 offset) Work Equip 01, with 14x6.5 in the rear. You can just catch a glimpse of the HKS Windmaster muffler out back.

(2) Mike Urbano's wife, Florabel, at the track practicing with his 1JZGTE-powered JZA70 Toyota Supra Twin Turbo. A recognized Supra guru in the Toyota community, Mike Urbano's 1991 Supra was known as one of the best JZA70/MA70 chassis Supras in the country, with several magazine features and car show awards. The car was featured in *SuperStreet*, *D-Car* in Japan, and several magazines in Europe, and won the most difficult classes at Import Showoff events. Though it was a show car, Mike always drove it at touge—he wasn't afraid to drive the car he had built.

Full Counter! Charlie Ongsingco from Full Counter Club was one of the better drivers in the early days, and he certainly had one of the cooler cars. His S13 Silvia is set up with the "classic drift look." His Silvia, which was nicknamed "DriftHeaven" because of his license plate, had an OEM Japanese Silvia front bumper with OEM zenki front lip spoiler (available in the United States on the 1989 S13 240SX) with non-projector headlights and the super cool "R32 style" grille. It was slammed super low, with 15x7.5 SSR/Precedeo demon camber wheels, which he bought from Kenta Ogawara at Alta Wheel Shop in Temple City, California.

D1 DRIVER SEARCH

June 15, 2003. Irwindale Speedway,
Irwindale, California

DRIFT DAY 6

July 5, 2003. Candlestick Park Parking Lot,
San Francisco, California

Drift Day 6 was the first-ever Drift Day event held in beautiful Northern California. For this event, we returned to the nice ocean breeze and sunlight of San Francisco's Candlestick Park, which was where some of us began driving.

(above) The Cipher Garage display at the Option Media booth, which was selling Japanese drinks, water, videos, and other miscellaneous drifting-related items. Also for sale at the booth were Speedwell shoes—the first time Speedwell had been marketed to the drifting crowd. The Cipher Garage kouki AE86 is seen here with kouki OEM bumpers and 14x8 SSR Mark III wheels. The framed Cipher Garage image on display at the booth was a digital painting of the author's AE86, done by Jeff Huang, a transportation design major at Pasadena's Art Center College of Design.

(above) The D1 judges just announced that 16-year-old Kenshiro Gushi qualified to drive in the first-ever D1 event, which would take place at Irwindale two months later. Incredibly proud of her son's accomplishment, Mama Gushi ran up in tears to give her son a hug while the Option crew captured it all on tape. In the foreground, you can see Charlie Ongsingco, Nobushige Kumakubo, Manabu Suzuki, and Kazuhiro Tanaka.

Alex Pfeiffer shows how he gets down with fellow BattleSwing teammate Gaylord Garcia's all-motor 1986 Corolla GT-S coupe, as Gaylord holds on for dear life.

DRIFT DAY 7
July 25, 2003. California Speedway
Parking Lot, Fontana, California

Drift Day 7 at California Speedway had two courses. One was for advanced drivers, the other for beginners. This is the starting line of the advanced course, with Apex'i USA's Len Higa entering the course in his white zenki S14. In the background, you can see the SC300 of Jensen Oda, also from Apex'i USA, Calvin Wan's FD, and the AE86s of Taka Aono, Wesley Hamachi, and Hiro Sumida.

(left) Old-school Toyota mechanic Roy Vizcarra accelerates out of the turn in his 1985 AE86 GT-S, which is a fully stripped out SCCA Solo2 competition car, equipped with a Cusco roll cage and fiberglass hood, Japanese zenki front bumper, and 15-inch Enkei 92 mesh wheels. Roy was well known in the Bay Area for being one of the top technicians at AutoPlus, a performance shop in South San Francisco that was the best at catering to the developing drifting and "JDM crowd" in the mid 1990s.

(right) Ken "Alta Ken" Ohara from Alta Wheel Shop (So-Cal Alteration) works on his first-generation Mazda RX7 in the pit area at California Speedway. The masking tape on the fender was a ghetto attempt at advertising "Alta Wheel Shop" on the side of Ken's RX7, but the non-sticky blue masking tape flew off while he was on track . . . and since he could hardly speak English, he had no clue that "weel" was not the right way to spell "wheel." In the background, you can see all the Drift Day stickers piling up on the side window of Kyle Mohan's first-gen RX7.

THE FIRST D1 GRAND PRIX IN THE USA

August 31, 2003. Irwindale Speedway, Irwindale, California

Nobuteru Taniguchi, also known as "NOB" (No One Better), takes a moment to relax, leaning up against the Yokohama Advan trailer. Taniguchi started out as a drifter, but eventually built himself up to become a professional racing driver in the GT300 class of the Japan GT Championship (JGTC). Originally from Hiroshima, Japan, Taniguchi gained recognition as the top drifter in his team, After-Fire, and began being featured in early drifting videos. He eventually moved to Yokohama, Japan, to pursue a career in racing, and began working for D1 driver Takahiro Ueno, who owns a race shop called Sui-Vax and the popular aero kit company, T&E (Vertex). He no longer works for Ueno, but the two remain good friends; in fact, Taniguchi lives directly across the street from Ueno, in an apartment that sits atop a Kentucky Fried Chicken restaurant in Yokohama, Japan.

(above) Andy Yen, leader of Swing Battle, and Roy Vizcarra return to the pits after an aggressive track session. Andy had just repainted his 1985 coupe a "UPS brown primer" color, and was representing his dad's shop in Walnut, California, with the "TB Auto" sticker on his windshield. Riveted below the GTS front lip is the "Home Depot SPL" garden trim front lip that became the trend for Southern Cali canyon runners. If you look through his grille, you can see a huge oil cooler, helps his 4AG engine stay cool—even under constant abuse at high rpm.

(right) Brandon Friedman (in the middle with the afro) from Swing Battle on the side of the track with his friends, waiting for their turn to run.

(below) **Try depositing this in an ATM. The first winner of the D1 Grand Prix USA, Katsuhiro Ueo with Yokohama's first U.S. race queens, Miho Nishimoto (left) and Sunisa Kim (right). Ueo was so joyful to have won the first D1 in the United States that he was crying right before he was presented with his trophy and a huge cardboard check. He seemed to calmed down a bit after seeing the check amount.**

(above) Ueo vs. Taniguchi. This was one of the most highly talked about tandem battles in the early days of drifting. Katsuhiro Ueo, owner of a small car shop called Sift from Kyushu (Southern Japan), drove his normally-aspirated AE86 Sprinter Trueno at the absolute limit to defeat the HKS Works S15 Silvia of Nobuteru Taniguchi. Taniguchi and Ueo were running extremely close together, regardless of the fact that Ueo's hachiroku only had a 200-horsepower 16-valve 4AG engine, and Taniguchi was pushing 500 horsepower with his SR20DET-powered S15. In the final run, Taniguchi followed Ueo super closely, but in the middle of the infield sweeper, he hit the outer wall, leaving Ueo to drift to victory. This tandem match proved to Irwindale's crowd of 10,000 spectators that the driver is the key to winning drift events, not high-horsepower machines.

The First Drift Showoff
March 2, 2003

Drift Showoff was the brainchild of Ken Miyoshi from Mainstream Productions, an early pioneer in the import aftermarket industry. Back in 1995, Miyoshi held the first Import Showoff car show at Pomona Fairplex in Pomona, California, catering to imports and sport compact cars only.

In January 2002, Miyoshi took a trip to Tokyo Auto Salon, and was invited by Signal Auto to the futou (bay side) street drifting spots in Osaka. It was then that Miyoshi met "Drifter X," Fumiaki Komatsu, a Signal employee who drifted in an RPS13 180SX. Miyoshi took a seat in Komatsu's 180, and Komatsu rocketed into the night, drifting all over Osaka's industrial bay area. Ken admits, "That was the night I got hooked into drifting. After that ride, I was like, man . . . I really gotta put together a drifting event in the U.S.A."

When he returned to Los Angeles, Miyoshi began planning Drift Showoff to elevate motorsports in the United States by doing something different from car shows and drag races.

During the initial stages of planning the first Drift Showoff, Miyoshi was introduced to Nick Fousekis, who had only recently begun working in the marketing department of Falken Tire Corporation in Rancho Cucamonga, California. After their initial meeting, Miyoshi met with Nick and his boss, Darren Thomas, who was very interested in getting Falken involved with drifting. After speaking to Miyoshi, Falken decided to become a major sponsor of Drift Showoff.

Ken explained, "Actually Nitto Tires was sponsoring the Signal team at the time, and I already arranged for Signal to be main cars in the show . . . but Nick had a good idea. He mentioned that they had two Falken-sponsored drivers in Japan, Yoshinori Koguchi and Seigo Yamamoto. Nick proposed that Falken could ship the cars to LA and fly the drivers in so they could do the demo. And the thing is, Koguchi is like the god of S13s! At the time, he was more respected and well known than any other driver that was gonna do a demo at Showoff."

Word spread quickly among fans that Japanese pro drifters would be coming to Irwindale Speedway, along with their real drift cars from Japan.. To make things even more interesting, the inaugural Drift Showoff would have an amateur drifting competition. And to assure that the first Drift Showoff had plenty of eye candy aside from just the cars, original Drift Showoff girls, Verena Mei, Ariel Rose, and Yu were on hand to take pictures with spectators. However, on this particular day, the focus wasn't on models—it was all about drifting. Ken recalls, "In the morning, when the Japanese drivers were doing their warm-up laps, everyone who was setting up and cleaning their cars in the car show section started trippin' out and calling up all their friends on their cell phones . . . and the lines at the gate got longer and longer! We had Jon Miranda at the gate letting people in, and it was so crazy! The lines were so long, some people waited for an hour and a half just to get in!" Driving Signal Auto's RPS13

"Strawberry face" Sileighty was "Drifter X," Komatsu. "DrifterXL," Kazuya Bai from Osaka's top team, Tinker, rocked Signal's S15 Silvia.

From the Falken team, Seigo Yamamoto brought his black and fluorescent yellow JZX100 Toyota Chaser, and street drifting legend Koguchi brought his red 180SX, famous in the Japanese drifting community because so many of Koguchi's fans tried to emulate his car's signature "Koguchi style." Ken explains, "I couldn't believe it. It was Koguchi's real car! When Koguchi got out there, he completely wrecked shop! He totally wowed the crowd."

For the amateur drift competition, a local drifter named Benson Hsu rose above 42 other competitors to win the first-place trophy, a set of Falken tires, a Bomex aero kit, and $500. More importantly though, he won the respect of his fellow competitors and was awarded the chance to drive tandem with his idol, Koguchi himself. By the end of the day, attendance at the first Drift Showoff reached 7,200 spectators.

DRIFT SHOWOFF
**October 12, 2003. Irwindale Speedway,
Irwindale, California**

Koguchi pulls the e-brake to adjust his
S13's slide angle as he closes in on
Seigo's S14 on the last sweeping turn of
Drift Showoff's infield course.

(above) A newcomer to the U.S. drifting scene, Swedish driver Samuel Hubinette proves that he can handle a car amazingly well as he comes off Irwindale's oval and accelerates through the wide sweeping left-hand turn farther infield. Even though the S14 he was driving was turbocharged, it looked nothing like a drift car, with vinyl stickers haphazardly stuck all over the car.

Piloting friend and team manager Jerry Tsai's first car, the Pacific Rim S13 Silvia, Daijiro Yoshihara rocked super-clean consistent lines in his elimination-round runs, coming closer to the inner retaining barrier than most of the other drivers. Dai ended up with a Drift Showoff podium finish. Rhys Millen took first in his JZA80 Supra twin turbo, second place went to Daijiro Yoshihara with the PacRim S13 Silvia, and third place was held by Taka Aono with his AE86 hatchback.

The crowd and media were all surprised to see an unknown driver competing in a brand-new Nissan 350Z, which made a whining noise as it passed, due to the supercharger under the hood. There weren't too many fixed-up 350Zs on the scene yet, especially not one that looked like this. The mystery driver was young Chris Forsberg, who had just moved out from Pennsylvania with nothing more than the keys to his 350Z and the dream of becoming a professional drifter.

Koguchi purposely loses a bit of momentum in his drift, so he can slow down and wave to the Drift Showoff crowd, but scrubbing speed doesn't seem to be a problem for a pro driver like him. As he continued through the turn, he re-initiated drift and flipped the car in the opposite direction for the next turn.

Katsuhiro Ueo might very well be the best AE86 drifter in the world. His driving style is admired by drifters around the world, including his own competitors in the D1 series. Ueo drifts at high speed, with high rpm and full commitment to the turn as he enters the corner, holding down the gas pedal and repeatedly kicking the clutch pedal to keep the drift going without slowing down.

DRIFT DAY 9

November 7, 2003. Las Vegas Motor Speedway, Las Vegas, Nevada

(1) D1 pro driver Yasuyuki Kazama was one of the first drivers in Japan to build up an S15 Silvia for drifting. He went deep into debt to build his first S15, which was bright red when the car was still new. His dedication and hard work paid off, as he earned a sponsorship by Kei Office (Keiichi Tsuchiya's brand of suspension) to drive in D1. Kazama and the Kei Office crew came to Las Vegas Speedway with the help of Clayton York of Autolink. Kazama is shown here doing a drift demonstration run in his Kei Office S15. Along with all the sponsor stickers (Bridgestone, Potenza, Nismo, Kei Office, etc.), Kazama and many of the D1 drivers run the private drift team stickers of their friends (Rough World sticker on the taillight, Rapid stickers on the bumper, and Drift Xtreme on the wing).

(2) Adam Matthews from Rancho Cucamonga, California, made the long drive out to Las Vegas in his gray S14, and was tearing up the track with his SR engine.

DRIFT DAY 9.5 (FOR INSTRUCTORS ONLY)

November 22, 2003. Irwindale Speedway,
Irwindale, California

DRIFT DAY 10

November 29, 2003. California Speedway Parking Lot,
Fontana, California

(1) J. T. Arranz from Full Counter Club attacks the first turn of the course—a sweeping left hander. You can tell he's on the throttle because the front of the car is lifting up, showing off the shiny lips on his 15-inch SSR Reverse Mesh wheels.

(2) Ko Kagiya throws Miki Ohkita's gold AE86 hard into the corner, with early Drift Day instructor and Solo2 competition Miata driver Kenji Sakai sitting shotgun.

(3) Sean Holloway from Apex'i USA has a beautiful street-legal R32 Skyline GT-R, which he brought out to Drift Day events and rocked out on the track! Notice the huge Apex'i intercooler peeking out from behind the bumper, and the dark gray Regamaster Evo wheels fully countered.

(4) When Steve Nakamura from Monterey Park, California, throws his AE86 into the corners, his Fujitsubo "Old Car Series" exhaust emits a cool throaty tone.

1

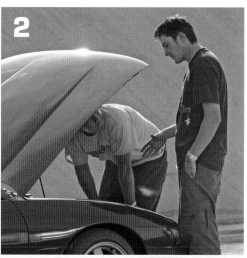

2

(1) Mark has a lot of experience in S13s, S14s, and turbos. He has been building S13s for a long time now, and built this whole car by himself, including the paint work. Mark was the first person in the United States to put an RB25 in an S13 for drifting. It's apparent that the car has ridiculous amounts of power! Mark needs to be easy on modulating the throttle, or else it won't hook up and just spins the tires.

(2) Mark Slide Squad explains his engine setup to Andy Yen while waiting to run the next group.

As the sun sets on the California Speedway, nothing could be more beautiful than the sound of squealing tires, screaming individual throttle bodies, and the whooshing sounds of turbos. Perfect.

(1) The Pacific Rim booth at the event had Hiraoka's Espelir AE86 D1 car on display.

(2) Jeremy Sakioka's S13 has hardly any body roll, even when he throws it hard into the corners. S13 coupes look best when they are super low to the ground, like this one.

(3) Ken Ohara from Alta was always breaking things on his RX7, but at least he always had good offset wheels, like the SSR XR-4 wheels seen here.

DRIFT DAY 12
Janaury 16, 2004. Irwindale Speedway
Irwindale, Californi

Chris "Chinky" Chau is one of the bad-boy members of So-Cal's SwingBattle drift team, with crazy spiked hair, piercings, and a cool S13 Silvia. Chinky used to work at Autolink as their tuning specialist for Apex'i PowerFC computers.

Drift Day instructor and Formula D star driver Casper Canul sits in Hawaiian drifter Len Higa's S14 to lend advice and share techniques on how to drift well. Casper's family owns the Mobil gas station on the corner of Valley Boulevard and New Avenue in Alhambra, California, and he always invites people to stop by for free drifting advice. Casper became the first Nitto Tires driver to achieve a podium finish, doing so at Formula D Round 1 at Wall Speedway, New Jersey, in 2005.

Geoff Wise, a student at Cal Poly Pomona, spends most of his free time driving his red 1985 GT-S coupe, or going to classic car shows with his 1966 Sunbeam Alpine and his dad.

The start line at Irwindale Speedway, with Irwindale's picturesque rock quarry in the background.

DRIFT DAY 13
February 20, 2004.
California Speedway parking lot,
Fontana California

When Andy Yen practices in Autolink's S13, everyone watches. The car always attracted so much attention because of the bright pink and red graphics and the monstrous sound of the wastegate when Andy was on the throttle.

There is nothing more fun than drifting, as Brandon Friedman's passenger so clearly demonstrates. Brandon's car is the typical canyon bomber Corolla. No frills, just skills.

Gloomy! Andy Yen tests out Clayton York's Autolink S13 in the rain. Andy eventually drove this car in D1 and the first year of Formula D, but the "Gloomy Bear" graphics didn't stay on the car long, unfortunately. Everything from the character, motion conveyed, and usage of color just made it so cool. Props to Clay on the original idea and design of this graphics scheme.

D1 GRAND PRIX USA
February 28, 2004. Irwindale Speedway,
Irwindale, California

Daijiro Yoshihara's best friend and mechanic, Masa, changes the wheels and tires on the
Pacific Rim S13 before Dai takes the car out for some practice runs.

(1) Kazuhiro "KFC" Tanaka of Team Orange attacks Irwindale's oval at super-high speed with his M-Sports S15 Silvia, built by Shigeru Ohki at tuning shop Tex Modify in Ibaragi, Japan. Tanaka is a member of the legendary drift team Rough World, the team that started a lot the cool drifting style trends for AE86s in Japan, like spray painting the wheels of the car black for a tougher look, using zipties on the fenders, and demon camber, which is also known as "oni-kyan." Demon camber is a slang term that describes incredible amounts of negative camber in the front wheels. The style was created mostly to make the cars look tough and aggressive; it's not necessarily more functional.

Apex'i driver Youichi Imamura was well-known in Japan for ripping through mountain roads in his brown AE86 Sprinter Trueno, but his D1 competition car is an FD3S RX7. Imamura is seen here doing testing runs at Irwindale, in his "T-car," the left-hand-drive twin of his Japanese Apex'i competition car. Imamura decided to use the 350-horsepower T-car for testing at Irwindale because he didn't want to risk his favorite D1 car (the 450-horsepower, right-hand-drive Apex'i FD3S) on Irwindale's banking and surrounding walls. Remember, drifting is just as much about style as it is about actual driving.

Since Calvin Wan had slammed his red FD3S RX7 hard into Irwindale's wall at a D1 event a few months earlier, he was still working on putting together a new FD for competition and didn't have a car to drive at the February 2004 D1 event. With the help of Toshi Hayama from Apex Integration in Orange, California, Calvin was introduced to the guys at Motorex, who let him drive the Motorex/Apex'i Z33 350Z for D1 Grand Prix. Toshi was integral to making this deal happen, making the introduction and personally endorsing Calvin as a driver. Toshi once said, "People always call Apex and ask us if we'll sponsor their cars, but I sponsor people, not cars. I like his attitude, and that's why I sponsored him."

One great thing about drifting events, especially events such as D1 Grand Prix and Formula Drift, is the level of crowd interaction and excitement generated! As exciting as other traditional motorsports may be, the crowd just doesn't seem to get as involved as they do at a drifting event. For motorsports-loving adrenaline junkies, drifting is absolutely hard to beat.

The view of the D1 course on event day from Irwindale Speedway's roof, high above the grandstands.

The Japanese D1 drivers put on an impressive display of tandem donuts, making the crowd cheer and stomp as they get sprayed in the face with all the tire smoke!

DRIFT DAY 14
March 28, 2004. Irwindale Speedway,
Irwindale, California

A long line of cars develops right outside the oval as drivers grid up for the next run group to hit on the course. Irwindale's oval is hot (there are cars running) and there is no entry or exit until the present run group stops running. Once the Drift Day course workers okay the change of run groups, the next line of cars can enter the oval and the old run group leaves.

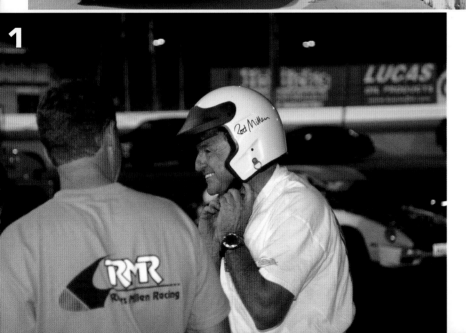

(1) Like father, like son. Rod Millen gets a taste of how fun drifting is when Rhys lets him take his GTO out at Irwindale Speedway. When Rod got out he had an ear-to-ear grin—drifting has that effect on people.

(2) Ryan Hampton, Jim Liaw, Andy Yen, and Motorex owner Hiro lean on Chris Forsberg's car, watching the practice runs at Irwindale. Chris was done running for the night; he had just shattered the windshield on his 350Z.

(3) For the first time, with everyone watching, Ken Gushi straddles the door of his S13, trying Kazama's famous "rodeo drift" move. However, Gushi's legs are too short, and he ends up bailing out of the car.

ROAD & TRACK INTERNATIONAL DRIFT SHOOTOUT

May 1, 2004. Laguna Seca Raceway,
Monterey, California

Rhys Millen impressed the crowd and judges with clean, consistent, smoky runs in his factory-backed, RMR-built Pontiac GTO. RMR is truly an innovator in the world of drifting. They took their experience in rally competition and race car preparation, and applied it to building a competitive drift car from a brand-new showroom-stock Pontiac GTO—a vehicle that had never been meant for drifting.

1

(1) The battle between drifting's golden child, Ken Gushi, and Rhys Millen was a fierce one indeed. Rhys certainly didn't make it easy for Ken, laying down perfect, consistent runs with plenty of angle and smoke. With the torquey V-8 engine under the hood of the GTO, entry speed and power to continue the drift certainly weren't problems. However difficult an opponent Rhys may have been, Ken showed no fear whatsoever, and entered the dogfight with Rhys with everything he had. To keep his speed up, Ken revved his SR until it could rev no more, and became one with his S13, winning the battle with a combination of driving skills, willpower, and guts.

(2) Overjoyed and at a loss for words, Ken Gushi accepts the first place award presented by *Road & Track* magazine and Yokohama Tires.

(3) Speechless and emotional with tears of joy, Ken's proud father, Tsukasa Gushi, ran up to the stage to give his son a hug, like any proud parent would . . . but this was no little-league baseball game that Kenshiro won. He just competed against some of the top drivers in the United States and came away with top honors, a check for ten thousand dollars, and the respect of all the drivers and media personnel who witnessed the historic event.

2

3

DRIFT SHOWOFF MIAMI AND MIAMI D1 DRIVER SEARCH
May 28–30, 2004. Homestead-Miami Speedway, Miami, Florida

Homestead-Miami Speedway, which typically hosts events such as NASCAR races, had just gotten its first taste of drifting. As the clouds in the sky offered temporary relief from the hot sun, they still didn't help with the heat and humidity.

(above) Ben Schwartz came down from Fort Walton, Florida, to compete in the event in his white S13 Silvia, which was without a doubt one of the best-developed S13s in Florida at the time. As Ben executes high-speed, smoky passes in front of the Miami crowd, it's easy to tell why he developed the nickname "Big Smoke."

After Drift Showoff's drift demo, fans crowded around the Falken pits to get autographs from J. R. Gittin, Calvin Wan, and Seigo Yamamoto, with Falken models Joyce Lex and Mary J. Castillo passing out tire flyers and promotional material in their casual clothes. Apparently their white vinyl "race queen" uniforms became just too hot and sticky in the humid weather.

1

2

3

(1) Florida resident Ben Schwartz accelerates through the back section of the track.

(2) When he heard that the Miami Drift Showoff would be combined with an East Coast D1 Driver Search, J. R. Gittin trailered his S13 Silvia all the way down from Maryland with the help of his dad, Vaughn, and rocked out at Homestead-Miami. The Japanese D1 judges, Keiichi and Nomuken, were impressed enough to grant him entry into D1. As he accelerates back up to the grid area, the polished lip of his 17-inch Buddy Club wheels almost touch the ground, and the tip of his Tanabe exhaust peeks out from behind the clouds of tire smoke.

(3) In the pit garages, Falken team mechanic Kevin Wells from LS Automotive hustles to replace the throttle body on J. R. Gittin's Silvia with one from Koguchi's 180SX, as his girlfriend patiently watches.

DRIFTING AT PIKE'S PEAK

June 25, 2004.
Pike's Peak International Hillclimb
Colorado Springs, Colorado

Team Falken's drift cars line the side of the road, just before the start line of the world-renowned Pikes Peak Race to the Clouds. At 3:30 a.m., there was already traffic from the hordes of early-bird spectators lining up to drive their cars up the mountain, camp out, and watch the cars ascend the mountain. Falken's drift cars pictured are (right to left) Seigo Yamamoto's S14 Silvia, Calvin Wan's Discount Tire S13 240SX, Vaughn Gittin Jr.'s S13 Silvia, and Yoshinori Koguchi's S13 180SX.

Calvin Wan in the red Discount Tire S13 and J. R. Gittin in the blue S13 Silvia drift up and down the paved portion of Pike's Peak, as excited spectators watch and cheer from the side of the road.

Japanese drifting legend Yoshinori Koguchi makes his return to the mountains, but this time in Colorado. Koguchi rocked high speeds and deep angles going up and down the mountain. In one spot, Koguchi came wide up a turn, and hung both of his wheels off the side of the mountain! From the sky, it looked like he was going to fall off the side of the mountain for sure, but he just stayed on the throttle, and one of the wheels caught, getting him out of that scary predicament. Seasoned from countless nights drifting the winding roads of his home mountain in Tochigi, Japan, it's safe to say that Koguchi left his mark on this mountain.

DRIFT SHOWOFF COLORADO

June 27, 2004. Pike's Peak International Raceway, Colorado Springs. Colorado

Neither rain, nor sleet, nor snow . . . will stop us from drifting. Just 30 minutes prior, it was a nice sunny day in Colorado, but all of a sudden rain started coming down in buckets, covering the track in water, and flooding the dirt parking lot, causing all the spectator cars to get stuck in the mud. Determined to put on a good show, Calvin Wan pulls on his driving gloves and says, "Hell nah, we always drift in the rain in Frisco [San Francisco]! I'm going out." After his demo, he recalls, "Dude, it was raining hella hard; the windows were fogging up like crazy, so I had to roll down the windows just to see where I was going."

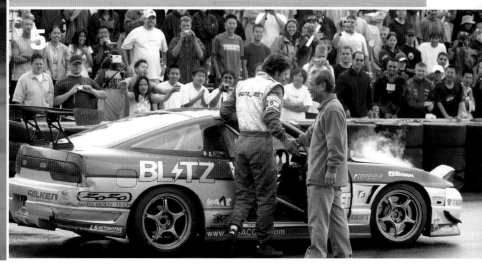

(1) Fresh after his ascent up Pike's Peak in his rally-prepared Pontiac GTO, Rhys Millen stops off at Drift Showoff in Colorado to do some demo runs, to the delight of the fans.

(2) Vaughn Gittin Jr. throws his S13 around the course, splashing around in the water and having fun.

(3) Looking for whatever they can find to stay out of the unexpected rain, a group of friends huddles underneath a 5Zigen wheel box.

(4) Calvin Wan lays a smokescreen of Falken rubber during a slow-controlled drift across the spectator area, much to the crowd's delight.

(5) "Ah gomen! Gomen!" exclaims a slightly embarrassed Koguchi, as he apologizes to Falken President Hideo Honda for blowing the motor during his drift demo. Lucky for Koguchi, Mr. Honda is pretty easygoing, and he just laughs it off.

FORMULA D DRIFT DEMO AT LAGUNA SECA CHAMP CAR RACE

**September 11, 2004. Laguna Seca Raceway,
Monterey, California**

Kenshiro Gushi and Dai Yoshihara joke around in Japanese while waiting for the other
drivers to join them on grid for their drift demo.

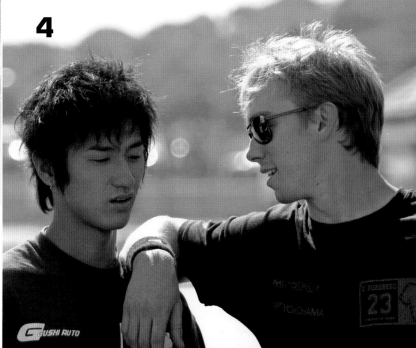

(1) The boys are back in town! Some of the top stars of the Formula D series, with the staff of Slipstream Global Marketing (left to right, third row: J. R. Gittin, Ken Gushi, Calvin Wan; second row: Andy Yen, Alex Pfeiffer, Jim Liaw, Tony Angelo Dai Yoshihara, Chris Forsberg; first row: Richard Tran, Fred Chang, Ryan Sage). Drifting is all about having fun! Formula D's young stars are enjoying the hell out of their tour experience.

(2) It has already begun. Ken Gushi concentrates on signing his name neatly on his hero (autograph) card as a young female fan waits eagerly.

(4) "Dude it'll be fiiine. Relax!" From the look on Chris Forsberg's face, he must be talking a young and impressionable Gushi into doing something he isn't too comfortable with!

(3) Laguna Seca's track map.

Ken Gushi and Dai Yoshihara manji (swing the tails of their cars back and forth, right to left) through the short straight underneath Laguna Seca's Bridgestone Tire bridge as they run backwards from Turn 4 and Turn 3.

(1) During the actual drifting demo at Laguna, many of the Champ Car fans got up on their feet, hooting and hollering from all the excitement of seeing the young drivers execute fully countered, smoky drifts across Laguna Seca's Turns 2, 3, and 4.

(2) Driving his car back to the pits, Kenshiro Gushi cheeses it up for the camera, more than happy to return to the track where he won top honors for the *Road & Track* International Drifting Shootout just four months earlier.

(3) Having just completed the drift demo, the drivers park their cars close together, and the crowd bum-rushes them, asking questions about the cars, drifting, and taking pictures.

NOPI SUPER SHOW AND AFTERPARTY

September 19, 2004. Atlanta Motor Speedway,
Atlanta, Georgia

Ain't no party like a DA party! At the bar in Atlanta, international photographer extraordinaire Fly from Max Power UK decides to party with the Drift Alliance guys, but J. R. decides to taste Tony Angelo's fingertips instead. Left to right: Fly from Max Power, Chris Forsberg, Vaughn Gittin Jr., Tony Angelo.

Inside the halls of the Nopi Super Show, Rich from the Drift Alliance camp stirs up the crowd with his wild antics and on top of that, someone gave him a bullhorn.

EA GAMES NEED FOR SPEED UNDERGROUND VIDEOGAME RELEASE PARTY

October 25, 2004. Irwindale Speedway, Irwindale, California.

A large crowd of drifting fans rush around Chris Forsberg's 350Z after the event, as Chris tries to clear a path to get back to the pits. He wanted to get his car out of there and away from the event stage as soon as possible, because rap star Snoop Dogg's unruly crowd of fans had just been released into the Irwindale infield. Like a swarm of bees, the new crowd jumped over the retainer barriers, swarmed the track and bum rushed the stage. The radio stations in Los Angeles were announcing a free Snoop Dogg concert at Irwindale Speedway, so what do you expect? The crowd got a little out of control.

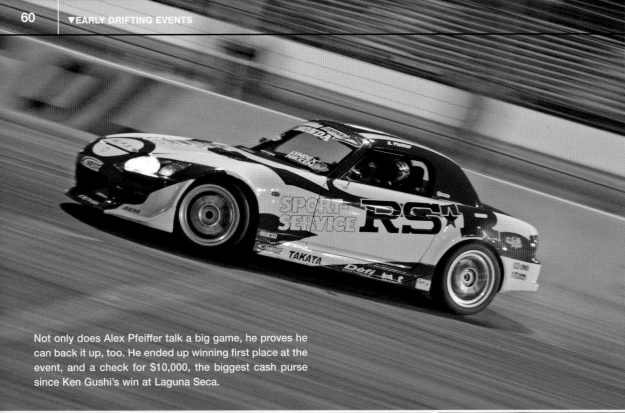

Not only does Alex Pfeiffer talk a big game, he proves he can back it up, too. He ended up winning first place at the event, and a check for $10,000, the biggest cash purse since Ken Gushi's win at Laguna Seca.

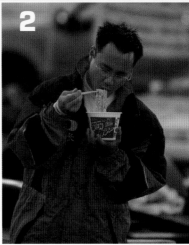

(1) The Motorsport Dynamics team from Sacramento, California (left to right) Henry Chung, Sam Cuirar, James Bondurant, Hubert Young, Bobby Brichetti, Zack Weiner, and James Young.

(2) Before the event, RS-R's Koji Ikeda gets down with instant ramen noodles instead of the traditional truck-stop quality junk food served at Irwindale.

(3) Falken umbrella girls Joyce Lex, Mary J. Castillo, and Courtney Day having a little fun clowning around on the track.

(4) Looking like she's up to no good, Falken umbrella girl Mary J. Castillo flashes the flirtiest smile while chillin' in the Falken pits before the first run.

MOTOR PRESS GUILD DRIFT DEMO

November 16, 2004.
Willow Springs International Raceway,
Rosamond, California

DRIFT SHOWOFF

November 20, 2004. Irwindale Speedway,
Irwindale, California

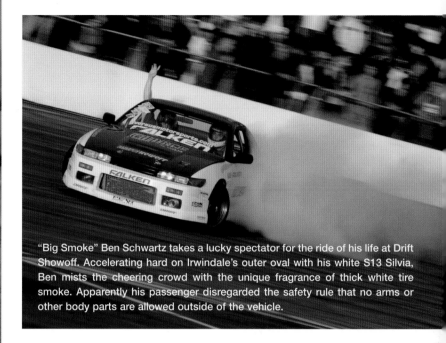

"Big Smoke" Ben Schwartz takes a lucky spectator for the ride of his life at Drift Showoff. Accelerating hard on Irwindale's outer oval with his white S13 Silvia, Ben mists the cheering crowd with the unique fragrance of thick white tire smoke. Apparently his passenger disregarded the safety rule that no arms or other body parts are allowed outside of the vehicle.

(below) Both of Falken star driver Calvin Wan's competition cars were on display for the members of the media. On the left, his newly built (and still unfinished in this photo) turbocharged Infiniti G35 for the 2005 series, and on the right, the Discount Tire S13 240SX that toured all over the country during the 2004 season. With the new G35 for the 2004 season, Falken Tire Corporation, driver Calvin Wan, and car builder Gary Castillo from Designcraft Fabrications all went down in history as the first drifting team to campaign a V35 Skyline (Infiniti G35) in drifting competition.

Drift Alliance top gun Chris Forsberg takes members of the automotive press on some drifting ride-alongs before he popped his motor at Willow Springs. Forsberg knows how to put an engine to its limits.

GT LIVE: D1 GRAND PRIX USA VS. JAPAN ALL-STAR MATCH
December 18–19, 2004. California Speedway, Fontana, California

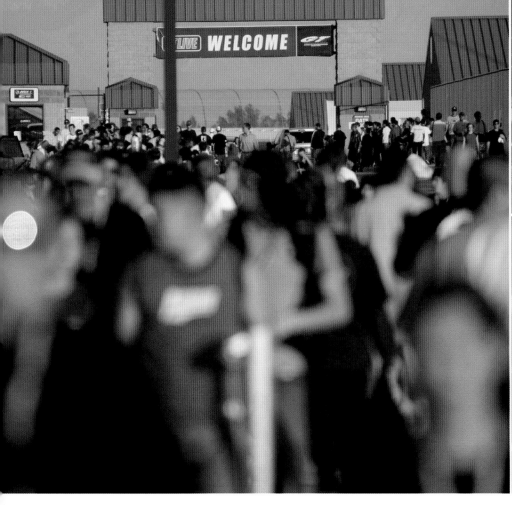

Quite a crowd gathered for 2004's GT Live Weekend, which included the JGTC All Star Race on Saturday and the D1 Grand Prix USA vs. Japan event on Sunday. There were a reported 30,000 spectators over the whole course of the weekend, and it certainly felt like it. It was difficult to move around in the pit area without bumping into someone. It was truly a spectacular event, combining the incredible machinery and professionalism of the JGTC series and excitement of a D1 Grand Prix drifting event, which is one of the most exciting spectator events in the motorsports world.

(1) Kumakubo wins! Team Orange's Nobushige Kumakubo jumps up and down excitement next to his S15 Silvia as the D1 announcers and judges stand to announce hi the first place winner of the D1 U.S. vs. Japan All Star match.

(2) Team Orange leader Kumakubo heads to the back section of the track, pulling his e-brak to change his line. His expertise in maneuvering his S15 Silvia yielded him top honors—a fir place podium finish at the first-ever D1 Grand Prix U.S. vs. Japan event.

Yokohama Advan Team gathered around D1GP USA vs. Japan winner Kumakubo. (Left to right, top row: Tak Masatomo, Sunisa Kim, Rhys Millen, Nobushige Kumakubo, Manabu Orido, Kazuhiro Tanaka, and Nobuteru Taniguchi; bottom row: Kristina Lew, Chad Harp, and Alex Pfeiffer.)

Ken Maeda (yellow) and Alex Pfeiffer (red) stop in front of the judges and get out of their cars to wave to the fans after their spectacular tandem battle.

Number One! Kumakubo gets rushed by international media trying to capture the victory shot, with him sitting on the carbon-fiber hood of his Ebisu Circuit S15.

DRIFT SESSION HAWAII
September 10, 2005. Hawaii Raceway Park, Hawaii

Justin Kikkawa initiates drift with a swift flick of the steering wheel and a kick to the clutch! This guy is a straight-up, hard-core driver; he enters the corners with full commitment and simply does not lift his foot off the gas pedal. Who cares if the car is a little banged up? Justin knows the right combination to make things work—demon camber, stretched tires with wide wheels, high entry speed, and deep angle.

(1) Paul Umholtz from Wahiawa, Hawaii, was involved in Hawaii's import drag racing scene in the early days, having raced an EG Honda Civic for a local shop, Hyper Sports. However, in 2004, things turned around for him. He began practicing drifting in his AE86 coupe, and eventually moved to an S13 Silvia. Paul insists adamantly that "drifting is totally better than drag racing. If I had known how much fun drifting was, I would have never started drag racing." He recalls filling up his gas tank before a Drift Session, and resetting his odometer to zero. At the end of the day, he checked the odometer and discovered that he drove 104 miles at the racetrack. Paul also had an interesting theory on drifting, explaining that, "drifting just has a better style element. Drag racing isn't as stylish, but drifting . . . it's like the motorsports equivalent of surfing—totally about style."

(2) Royce Fujimoto is a technician at Windward Toyota in his hometown of Kaneohe, Hawaii, and is well-known among the drifters on the island for his root-beer-brown metallic AE86 hatchback with 15x9 Work Equip wheels. He bought his Corolla in 2000 and began autocrossing, then started drifting in 2001. Royce stirs up attention when he drives because of his aggressive full-throttle driving style, which in the past has put his car into the wall at Hawaii Raceway Park. However, as soon as his car was fixed, Royce was back at it again, explaining that "drifting is so fun; it's kind of like a release. It's like being a kid again."

(3) Aside from Drift Session, Hawaii's island of Oahu has many beautiful and scenic roads to drive, like this stretch of the Kalaniana'ole highway.

Drift Session Hawaii

Far off in the middle of the Pacific Ocean, an interest for drifting was beginning to spark in Hawaii. In April 2001, Dave Shimokawa and Tom Bryant partnered up to create Drift Session.

They wanted to provide a positive alternative to illegal street racing along public highways and mountain roads. Drift Session's premiere event in April 2001 was the first event in Hawaii based on the sport of drifting alone. After the initial success, events were scheduled throughout the remainder of 2001, making Drift Session the first regularly scheduled drifting event series in America.

What made you decide to create Drift Session events?
The Drift Session was started from wanting to see if people were as good as they said they were. On Tantalus (the mountain road on Dahn), you can only see people drift one or two corners at a time, so your impression of them is very limited. You can hear tires screeching, but since you can't see so well in the dark, it's easy for anyone to claim that they're a good drifter. There were tons of stories about so-called drift kings, etc., out there that we wanted to see how good they were in broad daylight.

What was your reaction after organizing and experiencing your first Drift Session event?
I had heard stories about several of the guys that were supposed to be good, but just about all of them were really terrible; it was pretty much spin-outs and understeer all day long. At the first Drift Session, we must have had over 100 drivers participating, every one of them thinking that they were going to dominate the circuit. I think the first Drift Session was a very humbling experience for many. After that first event, people figured out that drifting was a little harder to do when people can see your every move. The second Drift Session event dropped down to somewhere around 15–20 drivers.

How have drivers evolved since then?
A lot of the initial crowd from the first Drift Session has dropped out of the scene. There were a lot of drivers though, who had a real hard time at the first Drift Session, but instead of getting discouraged and quitting, they were motivated to keep practicing and working to get better.

Justin (Kikkawa), for one, really started driving well after the first time he crashed his car. I remember seeing him on the road when I used to just cruise around in my own Corolla, and I remember thinking, "Man, that's the nicest Corolla I've ever seen." His AE86 was really nice back then, but after he crashed it seemed like he didn't really care anymore. So he went all out drifting. Justin once told me that he first decided to come out to Drift Session because he didn't want to be one of the guys with the really nice Corollas that didn't drive them. Justin is like the embodiment of the spirit of a true Drift Session driver. He just drives for himself. He is aggressive and hardcore when he drives. The competitive spirit is there, but that's not what it's all about. It's all about personal improvement and personal enjoyment. To us watching him, it seems like he drives with a lot of heart. Other drivers drive in our competition and they drive to win, but it's not emotional. It's more mechanical instead . . . but when Justin drives, its all heart, and all guts. He's like one of those "soul surfers" in Hawaii—the guys who don't go to surf competitions or try to get famous or anything, they just surf and do it for themselves. That's why like when Justin goes ripping around the track, people stand up and point him out and grab their kids and go, "Look! That's Justin!" It's not even that he has the nicest car or anything; he just stands out when he drives.

Which drivers are the stars of drift session?
Steve Oliberos - 2005 Group A Season Champ
Barry Wong - 2005 Group A 2nd Place, 2004 Season Champ
Shige Hirabayahi - 2005 Group A 3rd Place
My own favorite drivers to watch would be Shige Hirabayashi, Earl Huang, and Justin Kikkawa, because these guys never lift. They come through the high-speed corners with the gas pedal mashed to the ground. Once they initiate, they lock their wheel in place and floor it. It's like watching a kamikaze dive bomber.

Any specific milestones that are important to Drift Session or drifting in Hawaii in general?
April 2001, when Drift Session started running events. September 2002, Signal Auto came to Hawaii with Fumiaki Komatsu and their "Drifter X" 180SX. I feel that if anyone should be recognized for sparking the drifting craze that the U.S. has now its the guys from Signal Auto. At that time, our drivers had been drifting for over a year and thought they were already at the top of their game. By Signal Auto coming in and demonstrating what is possible with built vehicle and a good driver, everyone found themselves back at square one again.

credit: Jamm Aquino

Forrest Wang from Hawaii's North Shore has one of the cleanest S13 Silvias on the island of Oahu, and it was built mostly by his own hands. Rumor has it, it started out as an automatic CA18-powered car from Japan, but Forrest converted it and made it into the drift car it is today. His S13 has a lot of power, which helps him generate smoke and accelerate onto the straight on the back section of Hawaii Raceway Park.

(1) Shige Hirabayashi is one of Hawaii's best-kept secrets. He uses his S13 to the max of its potential!

(2) Barry Wong was one of the first drifters from Hawaii to get major sponsors like Yokohama Tires and Kaaz. He has a crazy reverse ice-cream-cone-looking exhaust tip.

Everyone who attended the event will agree that the most exciting drift battle was definitely between the muscular Mopar Viper Competition Coupe of Samuel Hubinette and the turbocharged AE86 Corolla GT-S of privateer Alex Pfeiffer, coated in flat black spray can primer.

In a spectacular display of aggressiveness and car control, the Viper and AE86 chased each other down Road Atlanta's hill and into the turns. On the first run, Alex's AE86 was in front, maintaining excellent speed, line, and angle through the turns, as Samuel turned the menacing Viper into a fixture on Alex's rear bumper. The growl of the Viper's V10 engine and the clouds of smoke billowing out of the Viper's rear fenders couldn't be anything less than intimidating. On the next run, roles were reversed. After a spectacular standing burnout, Samuel accelerated down the hill, leaving Alex's Corolla in the dust. However, undaunted and fearless, Alex chased after the Viper as fast as he could, and actually caught up to the Viper in the turns! The audience went berserk. Alex had caught up to Samuel and stuck it to him without hitting the other car. The judges couldn't decide. The judges and crowd chanted, "One more time . . . one more time. . . ." And the cars took off down the hill again, with Pfeiffer in the lead.

After the last run, the judges decided that Hubinette drove a cleaner line, by just a hair, and gave the victory to Samuel. The crowd went into an uproar, as the Atlanta locals seemed to develop a liking to Pfeiffer as the underdog—they wanted to see him win. However, there's just no contesting Hubinette's driving ability, and he continued to beat everyone else on the field for the first place trophy. Even though Pfeiffer eventually lost to Hubinette, the black primered Corolla still earned a place in everyone's hearts. To many, this was definitely the most inspiring tandem match of the event.

Calvin Wan, Falken Tire's first fully sponsored works driver in the United States, rocked clean lines with lots of tire smoke as he negotiated the horseshoe. Though Wan drives for Falken, Discount Tire was the title sponsor on the side of his car because of a marketing agreement between Falken and Discount Tire, one of Falken's biggest U.S. retailers. Discount Tire supplied these tires, wrapped around 17x9 (+15 offset) Racing Sparco wheels.

Blake Fuller from Braille Auto in Sarasota, Florida, shocked the crowd in Atlanta when he accelerated down the hill from the starting line in his Acura Integra! At first the crowd booed him, yelling "Front-wheel drive sucks!" When he entered the inner horseshoe at Road Atlanta, the crowd erupted, noticing his rear wheels spinning at a faster rate than the front, spitting out smoke from his rear fender wells, and a big smile on Blake's face. His Integra was rear-wheel drive! Nobody had expected anything quite like that.

(right) The competitors were staged on the hill at Road Atlanta, between Turn 9 and Turn 10A. The drivers lined up on grid and screeched down the track one by one for their qualifying runs, causing the trackside to smell like a mixture of suntan lotion and race fuel. Negotiating Turn 10A proved very difficult for most drivers because they weren't used to initiating drift on such a steep downhill.

Making the dirty south a little bit dirtier. Hiro Sumida takes Road Atlanta's horseshoe turn wide, dropping his rear right tire in the dirt! This technique is known as the "dirt drop drift." In actuality, it isn't really an initiation technique, but more of a drifting maneuver that is performed when the car is already in a state of drift.

Falken demo driver and Formula D judge Seigo Yamamoto shoots out of the horseshoe. His kouki (late model) S14 is outfitted with a DRFT aero kit and 5Zigen FN01RC wheels. 5Zigen is one of the most popular brands in grassroots drifting in the United States because of its numerous applications, ease of availability, and low cost.

Seigo Yamamoto makes the wastegate of his SR engine scream as he rockets back up the hill to Road Atlanta's starting line through thick clouds of tire smoke.

1

2

After all the media attention garnered by drifting's ever-growing popularity in the United States, there certainly was a lot of speculation concerning Formula Drift, the first professional drift series for United States drivers. Developed and promoted by Slipstream Global Marketing, Formula D's first round in the series brought a mixture of Japanese drifting culture and United States driving skills to Atlanta, the home of Coca-Cola and Freaknik.

(1) Even at the inaugural event of the Formula Drift series, Kenshiro Gushi of Team Rotora was already well known as the 17-year-old drift prodigy from San Gabriel, California, and one of the top drifters in the United States. His first claim to fame was qualifying to drive in the Japanese D1 Grand Prix professional drift series even before he received his California driver's license! Gushi explains, "I loved Atlanta. I especially thought it was so awesome that they opened the horseshoe turn on their track just for us drifters. That was really nice of them." He continued to say that he'd like to try driving the actual Road Atlanta track next time he's there, because it looked so fun.

(2) Ben Schwartz, a native of Florence, Kentucky, came all the way from Fort Walton, Florida, to compete in Formula D Round 1. Schwartz drove his S13 from Florida to Atlanta, and even Irwindale several times, loaded with tools and spare tires in the back, to compete in drifting events.

(3) Eiji "Tarzan" Yamada charges into the horseshoe's exit, with a huge American flag waving high above his black Dodge Viper, as he weaves in between Ryan Hampton's Mazdaspeed Miata and Akinori Utsumi's Motorex Z33 350Z during the pro driver demo. Formula D Round 1 was a milestone in the United States drifting history—it wasn't just any drift event. Being the first round of the inaugural professional U.S. drift series, this event was to go down in history.

(4) No, that isn't a neon kit. The blue glow and sparks from underneath the Braille Auto FR Integra is coming from a welding torch, which is precariously close to the gas tank of the car. Sparks igniting gas tank fumes could spell catastrophe to Blake Fuller, owner of the Braille Auto team. Fuller broke his axles during his last run, and the Braille crew had to repair them before he could run again the next day.

3

4

2004 FORMULA D ROUND 2: HOUSTON

June 12, 2004. Reliant Center, Houston, TX

Between the competition rounds, the Houston crowd was treated to tandem drift demos. Japanese pros Yoshinori Koguchi, in the Falken RPS13 180SX, took the lead, followed closely by Akinori Utsumi in the DRFT S13 Onevia, Seigo Yamamoto in the Falken S14 Silvia, and Tarzan Yamada in the Benihana/Team Taisan Viper Competition Coupe.

Team Toyo's Tony Schulz from Atlanta, Georgia, pulls the e-brake on his zenki (early model) Finishline Motorsports S14 to initiate a drift into the sweeping right-hand corner following the long straight at the beginning of the Houston course. Schulz has an IT background, but he no longer works in that field because he can't stop thinking about cars and drifting all day long. However, what he does have is natural driving ability—he's one of the top drivers from the DGTrials camp.

(1) The first thing on the agenda at Houston's Reliant Par was the driver's meeting. The heat was so blistering ever early in the day; most drivers were sweating through their T shirts and driving suits.

(2) Akinori Utsumi is a pro driver from Japan's Kansai area He is a member of the well-known Night Zone drift team which was made famous in Japanese drifting videos fo their five-car tandem drifts in matching teal blue metalli S13s and S14s.

(3) Fluent in both Japanese and English, Kenshiro Gush volunteered to serve as a translator for the judges durin the drivers' meeting. He used a bullhorn to shout ou instructions because Formula D drivers are a pretty rowdy fun-loving bunch—they get loud pretty quickly when yo have a bunch of them gathered in one spot.

(4) Formula D announcer Jarod "J-Rod" DeAnda interview racing legend Bob Bondurant. Of the new sport, Bonduran exclaimed, "Drifting is great. I just love drifting!" Bol Bondurant is a world-renowned driving legend. He raced fo Carroll Shelby, drove for the World GT Championship an Le Mans, and was handpicked by Enzo Ferrari to drive o Ferrari's Formula 1 team.

Falken driver Hubert Young drove the Motorsport Dynamics S13 brilliantly during his qualifying rounds at Houston, bringing the tail of the car so close to the barrier wall that the media could clearly see his sponsors' logos. At the time, he had a stable, good paying job as an internal accounting auditor for newspaper giant Knight Ridder. Young called in sick so he could make it to the Houston event.

Atlanta's Tony Schulz shows how it's done, accelerating toward the course exit in his yellow Zenki S14 240SX, nicknamed "Flying Banana" (not by Schulz). This S14 looks more like an SCCA road racing car than a drift car because of the styling and placement of the precut graphics. The bodywork is clean and simple, with just a front lip spoiler; most drift cars have dramatically aggressive aero bumpers, sideskirts, and mirrors.

Kenshiro Gushi broke his axles during practice the day before the Formula D event, but his hard-working dad, Tsukasa, and the determined Gushi Auto crew were able to get the car running again by competition day.

Erik Jacobs of DGTrials fame does a quick run-through of the course to test out the handling on his yellow S13 Sileighty. The car is jokingly referred to as "the ugliest S13 ever built" because of the painted JDM front grille, triple projector headlights, lack of corner lights and front lip spoiler, and huge positive offset wheels.

"Kakkoi desu yo ne!" exclaimed D1 drifting legend Nobuteru "NOB" Taniguchi, who visited Formula D in Houston as a surprise guest. Taniguchi was trippin' out on the amount of steering angle Rhys Millen's new Pontiac GTO could achieve! Millen admires Taniguchi as a driver, and despite a language barrier, the two top drivers have become good friends.

bert Young, a member of Team Symphonic, was getting crazy-deep angles out of his torsport Dynamics S13. Henry Chung, owner of Motorsport Dynamics, opened one he first import speed shops in California, and is one of the best builders of bocharged cars in northern California. Chung gets a lot of respect at track events ause he is extremely dedicated to supporting drifters, often sacrificing his personal e just to help people get their cars running well.

(1) Andy Yen rockets through the course sideways in the Autolink S13, built with Kei Office Suspension at Autolink Motorworks in Temple City, California. Autolink has close relations to many D1 drivers and teams. The week before D1 events at Irwindale, Autolink is always packed with Japanese D1 cars and has drivers and mechanics present trying to handle last-minute tuning issues.

(2) Houston's diverse crowd seemed to be melting under the sweltering heat of the sun, but they still stayed to watch drifting.

(1) Hiro Sumida's AE86 is built up old-school style. Awesome! It has OEM Japanese kouki (late model) bumpers with a zenki (early model) front lip spoiler and sideskirts. Sumida's car has super deep offset wheels sticking slightly out from the factory metal fenders, and the headlights glare aggressively. Sumida drives his AE86 like a champ, and has no problem keeping up with higher-power vehicles. It just goes to show that drifting is all about the driver, not necessarily the car.

(3) *D-Car* magazine's Japanese pro photographer Ogasawara brought out the big Canons for the event, making most of the other people with media passes look like amateurs.

(2) Holding a Kei Office umbrella above her head, Autolink's super-hot unofficial umbrella girl Nicole steps away from Andy Yen's car as he prepares to launch. An SCCA official gives him last-minute instructions before he enters the course.

(4) Slipstream's Andy Luk, affectionately known by Formula D staff as the "Dirty Panda," makes his way toward an impromptu discussion involving Jim Liaw, Richard Tran, and an SCCA official. Meanwhile, SCCA Solo2 National Champion Taka Aono prepares himself to go up against the battle-scarred and -bruised flat-black Corolla of Alex Pfeiffer, northern California mountain road champion.

Still in mid-drift, Eiji "Tarzan" Yamada leads Akinori "Ucchi" Utsumi off the course and into the pit area after their exciting display of tandem drifting, leaving the crowd on their feet and cheering for more.

Alex Pfeiffer riles up the crowd at the far bleachers during his practice runs. His 1985 turbocharged Corolla GT-S was custom painted by a friend just prior to the D1 Grand Prix event in February 2004.

Ernie Fixmer tries to find relief from the sweltering heat inside his Team Rotora S13 Silvia as he waits in line to run. Well-recognized as one of the United States' early drifting stars, Ernie was one of the first American drivers to earn the opportunity to run at the first D1 event in August 2003.

1

2

Vaughn Gittin Jr. watches his fellow drivers run as he waits in line wearing his thick driving suit, and a wet mechanic's rag on his head—Houston was that hot. Since Falken didn't appreciate the "wet rag look," they eventually hired more umbrella girls to be with the drivers as they waited on the track.

(1) Onetime! Most street racers shift into neutral as soon as they see a Ford Crown Victoria like this one because cops are always pulling over kids for having loud exhausts . . . but this is no ordinary cop car! This is a "Cobra Vic" from the Bondurant School of Performance Driving in Arizona.

(2) Terence Jenkins and Russell Naftal from Team Lateral G Racing do some last-minute fine tuning on Samuel Hubinette's Mopar Viper Competition Coupe before he begins his practice runs.

(3) The Pacific Rim Apparel booth was packed all day and proved popular for Houston showgoers who wanted to lace themselves up in the latest in motorsport fashion. Or maybe they just wanted to hang out in the shade. Good thinking, Pacific Rim.

Pacific Rim's Daijiro Yoshihara had an exciting, close-quarters fight with Chris Forsberg's 350Z, but in the end, Forsberg advanced to the final rounds.

Driving the Jasper Performance JZA80 Supra, Tyler McQuarrie is all over Ken Gushi as they maneuver around the long, sweeping right-hand turn at Reliant Center. A fearless Gushi keeps his line steady and wins the match, moving on to the finals.

3

4

(4) Driving his turbocharged blue S13, Ken Gushi tries to follow Calvin Wan in the Discount Tire S13 as closely as possible as they head toward the course's last turn during their tandem match.

(1) In between the concrete k-rails and chain link barrier fences, Slipstream's Fred Chang walks back into pit lane by himself, exhausted from the heat and a long day of shooting photos.

(2) As darkness fell, Taka Aono and Hiro Sumida's engines roared at full throttle, with headlights glaring as they battled each other, man to man, 86 to 86. It's inspiring to see two AE86s dancing together on the tarmac.

(3) SwingBattle versus BattleSwing. They might have been roommates back in the day, but Andy Yen and Alex Pfeiffer put all the familiar pleasantries aside and fought hard in their tandem battle. Though good friends, Yen and Pfeiffer have a friendly rivalry between them, and for this fight, bragging rights were just as important as advancing to the next round.

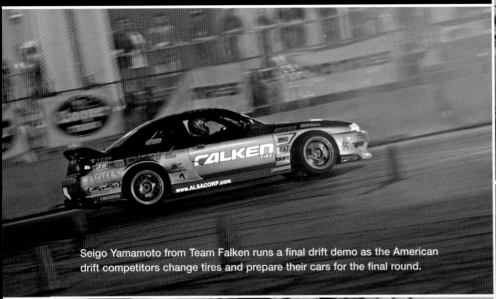

Seigo Yamamoto from Team Falken runs a final drift demo as the American drift competitors change tires and prepare their cars for the final round.

Samuel Hubinette and Ken Gushi went head-to-head in the final tandem competition for first place, but Gushi's rear axles snapped due to all the abuse they'd taken, and Ken was unable to finish. He couldn't locate and swap axles in the allotted time given by Formula D, so Mopar's Samuel Hubinette was declared the first-place winner and Gushi got second.

(right) At the trophy presentation ceremony, the media crowds the three winners, who shake their champagne bottles and pop the bubbly. However, someone at Formula D has screwed up and bought pink champagne, which turns the winners' hair and driving suits into a nasty pink mess. Samuel Hubinette (center) received first place, Ken Gushi (left) got second place, and third place went to Chris Forsberg (right). The Yokohama Tire Corporation was extremely pleased to have an all-Yokohama podium, and Forsberg and Hubinette were extremely happy to have each won two consecutive podium finishes at the first two rounds of Formula Drift. Hubinette might have been a bit happier than Forsberg, though; he won first place both times.

2004 Formula D Round 3: Sonoma

July 9, 2005. Infineon Raceway,
Sonoma, CA

Daijiro Yoshihara from Hachioji, Japan, and Rhys Millen from San Juan Capistrano, California, have an exciting battle as Yoshihara executes flawless runs and Millen stays right with him throughout the course. More than anything, tandem battles like this are what draw people to drifting events.

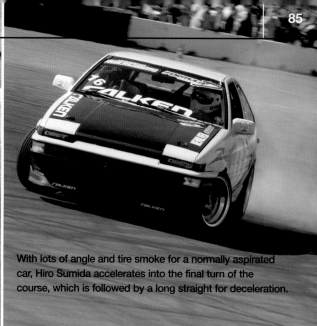

With lots of angle and tire smoke for a normally aspirated car, Hiro Sumida accelerates into the final turn of the course, which is followed by a long straight for deceleration.

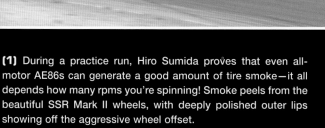

From the intense smoke, Daijiro Yoshihara proves victorious in his Pacific Rim S13 Silvia.

(1) During a practice run, Hiro Sumida proves that even all-motor AE86s can generate a good amount of tire smoke—it all depends how many rpms you're spinning! Smoke peels from the beautiful SSR Mark II wheels, with deeply polished outer lips showing off the aggressive wheel offset.

(2) Tsutomu Maehara from the Bay Area's Team Symphonic accelerates into the final corner of the course in his daily driven zenki S14. A mild mannered sushi chef by day, he turns crazy when he and his car attack the mountains. Maehara's favorite Japanese drifter is Ken Nomura (Nomuken) from southern Japan's legendary drift team FNR (Fukuoka National Racing).

(3) Dirt drop drift! Alex Pfeiffer comes wide into Sonoma's first decreasing radius right-hand turn. The rear tires of his flat-black Corolla drop in the dirt, resulting in his rear end slipping out, giving him even more angle. Beat up and battle scarred, the AE86 really lives up to the Battle Version moniker—no glitz, no carbon hood, no Japanese bumpers . . . hell, it doesn't even have a rear bumper! What it does have, however, is a skilled driver. Respect that.

(4) Henry Chung from Motorsport Dynamics generously offers to help Chris Forsberg fine-tune the ECU on his SR20DET-powered Nissan 350Z after Forsberg discovers his car won't start, which had worked just fine during practice. Frustrated, Forsberg scrambled to figure out what he would be driving in competition that day.

(5) Charlie Ongsingco of early drift team Full Counter Club was present at the event in his S13 Silvia. Ongsingco is responsible organizing private drift events called Just Drift, a place where higher-level amateur drivers can improve their skills.

(1) After a third-gear feint into the first right-hand sweeper at Sonoma, Drift Alliance frontman J. R. Gittin downshifts into second gear just before he reaches the next apex, using the momentum to accelerate out of the hairpin corner and laying down some good smoke as the crowd goes bananas.

(2) Drivers like Andy Yen are good examples for younger drifting enthusiasts. Even though Yen first developed his skills by attacking Southern California's canyon roads in his AE86, he always encourages young drifters to stick to safe events like Drift Day, where drivers can develop their skills much faster in a controlled environment with instruction from other drifters.

(3) Chris Forsberg drove the DRFT PS13 Onevia that Akinori Utsumi used for his demo runs because Forsberg's Z33 350Z was not running by the start of the competition. This was Forsberg's first experience driving right-hand drive in competition.

(4) Derrick Rogers, driving the Bubba Drift El Camino, is a crowd favorite at Formula Drift events even though his weapon of choice isn't a turbocharged Japanese car with a full aero kit. Instead, Bubba Drift chose an automatic Chevrolet El Camino with close to stock suspension and a big muscular V-8 engine. This car is a crowd pleaser without a doubt! All the car needs is some longhorns ziptied to the hood to complete the look!

1

2

3

(3) Swedish professional stunt driver Samuel Hubinette proves himself every time he gets into his Mopar-sponsored Dodge Viper Competition Coupe. He was a dominant force in the first year of the Formula D Championship.

4

5

(1) Down and dirty! Media favorite Rhys Millen from Team RMR got a little bit too aggressive during his final tandem run against Calvin Wan, who had to drive teammate J. R. Gittin's Falken S13 Silvia after Calvin's Discount Tire S13 suffered from broken axles. They say "rubbing is racing," but car-on-car contact is not the ultimate goal of tandem battles. The idea is to follow the leader as closely as possible without touching or forcing the leader to go off the intended line.

(2) No stranger to Infineon Raceway, Alex "Battleversion" Pfeiffer used to work at the track's Russell Racing School when it was still called Sears Point Raceway. A definite Bay Area favorite, he decided to rile up the NorCal crowd by doing his version of the "rodeo drift," a tricky exhibition technique invented by D1 driver Yasuyuki Kazama. To perform this move, Pfeiffer modulates the gas pedal with his foot, controls steering with his right hand, and uses his right leg to balance himself and hang on to the car. Kids, definitely do not try this at home.

(4) A frustrated and disappointed Ko Kagiya from Torrance, California, waits for the tow truck to escort his friend Miki Ohkita's beautiful gold AE86 coupe to the pits. Kagiya made minor contact with the wall, rippling the rear quarter panel of the car. Kagiya and Ohkita are members of a drift team called "Revvin Over 40's," a team whose members are all over 40 years old.

(5) During a special photo shoot taken while the drivers were on a break, Vaughn Gittin Jr. uses his Kaaz limited-slip differential to convert Falken rubber into thick clouds of billowing white smoke.

1

2

3

(1) Three-peat! Mopar's Samuel Hubinette proves himself the dominant force in the Formula Drift series as he wins his third consecutive first-place trophy at a Formula D event. Pacific Rim's Daijiro Yoshihara captures second place, putting him on the podium for the first time, and San Francisco native Calvin Wan wins third place in his hometown, marking the first time a Falken driver has ever achieved a podium finish. This time, the boys at Formula D get the right type of champagne, too.

(2) San Francisco native Calvin Wan put it down on his home turf, as he rocked clean, smoky runs in front of his Bay Area friends and family, who were scattered among the huge audience. It just goes to show, there are a lot of drifting fanatics in Northern California, but unfortunately there are not enough drifting events to go around.

(3) Import drag racing icon Stephan Papadakis made his official drifting debut at Formula D Round 3 in his yellow AEM-sponsored S13, causing quite a lot of talk about "big-time import drag guys entering our sport." Papadakis squashed all that immediately with his excellent attitude and willingness to learn from more-experienced drivers.

Team Falken celebrates its first Formula D victory.

(3) BattleSwing cofounder Hiro Fujita's zenki Levin two-door reveals a 4AGZE engine under the hood. The 4AGZE is the supercharged version of the AE86's original 1,600cc twin-cam 4AGE engine. The "4" in the engine designation indicates the size of the combustion chamber, the "A" is the engine series, the "G" indicates it's a twincam head, the "Z" is Toyota's designation for a supercharger, and the "E" is for fuel injected. This engine was available in the United States in the hard-to-find 1988 and 1989 AW11 Mr2 Supercharged. Fujita's front end is that of a Japanese OEM Corolla Levin, which does not have pop-up headlights like the AE86 Corolla GT-S in the United States. While an AE86 Levin was brought to the United States by Toyota Racing Development in the mid-1980s when the car was still new, the Levin-faced AE86 was not approved for export to the United States because the headlights were not physically tall enough U.S. Department of Transportation requirements. Nissan's S13 Silvia had the same issue.

(1) Calvin's trophy is the perfect size for his new puppy, Manji. Even the name of his dog evokes drifting. The Japanese drifting term manji refers to the movement of cars swaying side-to-side on a straight section of racetrack.

(2) Sure, Forsberg prefers tight jeans, vintage aviator glasses, and black Ramones T-shirts when he's off the track, but when he's in his office, he rocks nothing but Louis Vuitton.

(4) Nothing can be more fun than catching air on someone else's golf cart! The Drift Alliance guys know all about cars and weight transfer. They transferred all their weight to the back of the golf cart so they could get air, even though J-Rod and Andy Yen are up front. On the back of the cart, we have Chris Forsberg, Tony Angelo, Ryan Hampton, J. R. Gittin, and Alex Pfeiffer.

2004 Formula D Round 4: Irwindale

August 29, 2004.
Irwindale Speedway, Irwindale, CA

Chris Forsberg accelerates out of the last turn at Irwindale's inner oval, burning up his Yokohama rubber with his new gunmetal Volk TE37 wheels spinning furiously in the rear.

(3) James Bondurant of Phoenix, Arizona, exhibits incredibly clean, smooth runs in the Motorsport Dynamics S13 240SX. Bondurant was the first American to train at Dori-Goya, D1 tandem drifting master Nobushige Kumakubo's legendary drifting school at Ebisu Circuit.

(1) Samuel Hubinette flashes the peace sign from inside his monstrous Mopar Viper, which has a strong steel skeleton and lightweight carbon fiber skin.

(2) These taillights are all a person would usually see if they were trying to compete with Samuel Hubinette on a road race circuit. Mopar's Iceman waits at the starting line, waiting for the signal to charge off into the night.

1

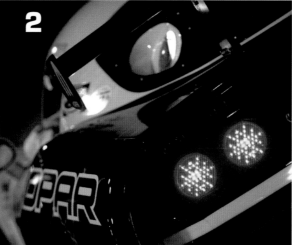

2

3

Victory! RMR's Rhys Millen screams in triumph. This marked Millen's first win in the Formula D series, and the first drifting win for RMR's sponsor, Pontiac.

2005 Formula D Round 1:
New Jersey
April 16, 2005. Wall Speedway,
Wall Township, NJ

Conrad Grunewald pilots the Motorsport
Dynamics S14 (which, incidentally, is Hubert
Young's own car that was loaned to
Motorsport Dynamics) in an intense battle
with Rhys Millen. Millen is a strategic driver
who is always looking for an opportunity to
pass or make his opponent slip up.

1a

1b

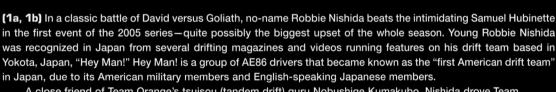

2

3

(1a, 1b) In a classic battle of David versus Goliath, no-name Robbie Nishida beats the intimidating Samuel Hubinette in the first event of the 2005 series—quite possibly the biggest upset of the whole season. Young Robbie Nishida was recognized in Japan from several drifting magazines and videos running features on his drift team based in Yokota, Japan, "Hey Man!" Hey Man! is a group of AE86 drivers that became known as the "first American drift team" in Japan, due to its American military members and English-speaking Japanese members.

A close friend of Team Orange's tsuisou (tandem drift) guru Nobushige Kumakubo, Nishida drove Team Orange's famous "Silvia K-Truck," supported by sponsors such as Falken Tires and Overboost, in U.S. competition. The K-Truck is a right-hand-drive Nissan 180SX, which was customized at Kumakubo's famous car shop, K-Style, with an S13 Silvia face. The back half of the car was removed to convert the 180SX hatchback into a truck. Kumakubo wanted to make a Japanese car emulate the vehicles in the NASCAR truck series he loves so much, along with all things American, such as Ford, GM, and Mopar.

However, when Mopar's blue and white met Orange in New Jersey, there were some unexpected results. Nishida drove the K-Truck (which the Formula D announcer called the "Sil-Camino") like he stole it, super fast and high into Wall Speedway's steep oval banking, with Hubinette's Viper right behind, breathing heavily on the K-Truck's rear bumper. As the announcer, J-Rod, yelled his trademark "Send it!" the pair rocketed back on track for another run, with Hubinette in the lead this time.

The battle was fierce indeed, but when the duo made their way to the course's inner horseshoe, Mopar's mighty Iceman came in with too much speed, driving his line rather wide. Seeing this split-second opportunity from behind a windshield littered with sponsor decals, Nishida went for it and took the inside line, positioning the nose of the K-Truck almost up against the Belle-1/Formula D Jumbotron screen, passing the Viper in mid-drift.

The crowd went absolutely insane. Who would have thought that some "no-name" AE86 driver could ever beat the unbeatable Samuel Hubinette! It was amazing. It just goes to show that the underdog does win every once in a while, even up against a driver of Hubinette's caliber and reputation.

(2) There was a huge crowd gathered at New Jersey's Wall Township despite the cold, windy weather and ambiguous Mapquest directions.

(3) On the grid, Gary McKinney discusses some things with McKinney Motorsports driver Ernie Fixmer as.

Media darling Ken Gushi pushes his Mustang, hot on the tail of Casper Canul's Monstor Fabrications S14, as they head toward the final set of turns on the Wall Speedway infield course.

Hubert Young from NorCal team Symphonic puts on a dazzling smokescreen in the Discount Tire S13.

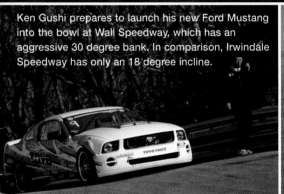

Ken Gushi prepares to launch his new Ford Mustang into the bowl at Wall Speedway, which has an aggressive 30 degree bank. In comparison, Irwindale Speedway has only an 18 degree incline.

1

2

3

4

(1) Daijiro Yoshihara looked good on the oval, driving an S13 (formerly Stephan Papadakis' Formula D competition car) borrowed from his friend R. J. DeVera. The car had Nitto Tires banger stick balloons sticking out of his trunk. Tracks usually don't allow cars with balloons, but this is drifting, so it isn't a problem.

(2) Brendan Walker from San Diego, California, lets a little tire smoke peel off his kouki S14's 5Zigen FN01RC wheels as he passes around the judging platform and into the last few turns of the course.

(3) One of the most anticipated cars being debuted at the first round of the 2005 Formula D series, Samuel Hubinette's Mopar Viper made the crowd howl in approval of its growling V-10 engine and the gobs of Yokohama rubber being annihilated by his rear wheels.

(4) Rhys Millen brings his monstrous GTO up close to the wall on the acceleration banking.

2005 Formula D Round 2: Atlanta

May 7, 2005.
Road Atlanta, Braselton, GA

When Rhys Millen and Vaughn Gittin Jr. go head-to-head in tandem competition, huge trails of smoke follow them. These V-8-powered modern muscle cars might not have been originally intended for drifting, but they have fared well in competition, giving the Japanese imports a run for their money.

Driving the Bubba Drift "Hell-Camino," Mike "MikeSpeed" Peters from College Station, Texas, stirs up attention with a combination of his long sideburns and a 330-horsepower, aluminum pushrod, LS1 V-8 engine.

(5) Ross Petty, one o Hawaii's top drifters, was a profiled driver in early volumes of Grip Video DVDs. He originally learned to drift in Okinawa, Japan, and moved from Hawaii to Southern California t drive the Rotary Power FD3S RX7.

(1) Daijiro Yoshihara from the Pacific Rim Drift Team powers out of Road Atlanta's horseshoe in his Charge Speed aero-kitted S13 and prepares to accelerate back to the starting line.

(2) Korean tire manufacturer Kumho Tires made a big mark on the drifting scene when it introduced "red smoke" tires, which were made by adding a pigment to the rubber compound while the tires were being produced. Two S13 drivers from Florida-based Enjuku Racing, Matt Vassallo and Rob Fleming, deputed the tires, which were discontinued because Formula D rules state that all tires used in the series must be full production tires.

(3) Spectators piled into Road Atlanta by the truckloads even though they had to sit on dirt. Some fans brough their own chairs and coolers to the event—very smart.

(4) AE86 driver Hiro Sumida is still getting used to his newly built right-hand-drive JZX90 Toyota Chaser, and puts his newly painted car and super-expensive Fina Konnection aero kit in the rocks.

(6) Team Finish Line driver Tony Schulz, a former IT gu from Atlanta, understeers past the entrance to Turn 10/ and slides into the dirt and rocks, busting up his bran new AIT aero kit, much to car owner Sae Kang's disap pointment. Tony is usually very consistent and definitel one of the best drivers in the Atlanta region.

There was quite a bit of controversy regarding the judging of some of the tandem runs, especially that of Taka Aono's AE86 and Samuel Hubinette's Viper. While some were happy to see the Iceman back on top of his game, some protested the judges overusing the "One More Time" clause because they couldn't reach a decision as to who won the intense and exhilarating battle. After three additional rounds of "One More Time," Aono was forced to withdraw because his car was overheating due to too many consecutive runs.

Driving his SR20DET-powered FD3S RX7, Seigo Yamamoto understeers in the horseshoe as he attempts to follow Kenshiro Gushi, who skillfully maneuvers his Ford Racing–sponsored Mustang with a good line and angle throughout the course.

1) Smoke rolls off the back tires of the Discount Tire S13 when Hubert Young is behind the wheel. Hubert might earn a good living as a licensed CPA, but he lives to drift.

2) East Coast S13 driver Mike "Carluch" Edwards tears it up at Road Atlanta with an aggressive e-brake initiation and cool-looking stock JDM front end. Even though Carluch drove this S13 for most of the 2005 season, the car actually belongs to his friend Rudy, who was a customer of Carluch Motorsports, a shop Edwards operated out of his garage in New Jersey. Carluch admits that not only did he drive this S13 in competition, he had to drive the car to and from each event, no matter where it was in the United States.

3) Dai, we have good news and bad news. The good news is that G4 Television's hot show host Mayleen Ramey is giving you a kiss. The bad news is that G4's not-so-hot creator of Formula D TV Josh Krane is, too.

New team driver Tanner Foust gets some serious angle in the McKinney Motorsports S13.

Every once in a while, even Rhys Millen ends up in the dirt.

2005 Formula D Round 3: Houston

June 11, 2005.
Reliant Center, Houston, TX

Kenshiro Gushi keeps right up against Conrad Grunewald's fender as the pair tandem through the last turn of the course in the finals.

Tanner Foust keeps his McKinney Motorsports S13 right up against the fender of his roommate Rhys Millen's GTO. In the background, the G4 Television camera crew expertly follows the cars, filming all the action for the next episode of Formula D TV.

When Tyler McQuarrie accelerates before the transition, the rear end of his Jasper Performance JZA80 Supra squats to put the power to the ground, spinning its Enkei NT03 racing wheels violently. When accelerating in a high power car like this, the driver needs to be accurate with the pedal pressure. Not enough pressure on the gas pedal will cause the car to lose momentum; too much pressure on the pedal will cause the car to squat down and do a burnout, which is what caused Mike Peters in the Bubba Drift El Camino to slam right into the Supra's expensive bodywork.

Calvin Wan swings his Falken G35's tail as he transitions from left turn to right.

Rhys Millen almost slams into the back of Seigo Yamamoto's SR20-powered RX7 as Seigo slows down and hits a cone entering the left turn in front of the judging stand.

The First Family of Drifting. Proud father Tsukasa Gushi, Mama Gushi, Kenshiro, and sister Hikaru cheese it up for the camera after Ken wins first place in his new Ford Mustang.

Al "Truenocoupe" Lagura drives his orange Techno Toy Tuning AE86 coupe past the judging stand, modifying the Rockford Fosgate/Drift Alliance foam hands with zipties to make his own personal statement. Don't think we didn't notice, Al. We love you, too.

This is what happens to wise guys like Al; the wise-guy act ends up coming back to bite you in the ass—or in this case, on the left side of your AE86. In a post-race interview, Al claims that he accelerated hard entering the course, but hit the bump in the middle of the track. He went airborne toward the wall, making him unable to steer the car. To avoid smashing the front of the car into the wall, he steered away, which saved his car, but damaged the wheels and suspension (control arms and both front strut spindles) pretty badly.

(1) After a hot day of driving, Ross Petty hangs out on the sidelines dressed in his team Boso attire, looking straight up Okinawa style.

(2) Winner's podium: Ken Gushi (Ford Racing Toyo Mustang,) first place; Conrad Grunewald (Motorsport Dynamics/Falken S14), second place; Rhys Millen (Pontiac RMR GTO), third place.

Samuel Hubinette topless in the Viper, revealing a full roll cage.

2005 Formula D Round 4: Sonoma

July 9, 2005.
Infineon Raceway, Sonoma, CA

Driving his supercharged Ford Mustang, J. R. Gittin from Drift Alliance attempts to erase Mopar strongman Samuel Hubinette from the picture by burning up his Falken Azenis RT615 tires, making it difficult for Samuel to see or breathe during their tandem bout.

Jay Lapid, who co-founded Graphtech Signworks with Calvin Wan in Daly City, California, had a minor incident at Sonoma with his S13, but was able to bandage the problem right away.

(1) Kenji Yamanaka, a Japanese driver from the Tokyo area always appears in Japan's *Drift Tengoku* Magazine. He began driving for Rotora in 2005, and always has a good presence on the track, even though he insists on wearing a crazy top hat and cape when he's off the track. Nandayo Yamaken!

(2) The crowd at Sonoma had an excellent view as Drift Alliance teammates J. R. Gittin (Falken Mustang, in front) and Tony Angelo (Falken RX7, following) initiated drift far before the "turn-in point" of the decreasing radius right-hand sweeper at Sonoma.

(3) Role reversal! Falken's Chris Forsberg gets his S15 stuck on the rumble strips when drifting meets rally, and Bubba Drift's Mike Peters, who Forsberg always complains about for being slow, is forced to slow down his Hell Camino to avoid slamming into Forsberg's S15 Silvia.

(4) Jay Yoshida and Scott Toshima from Schikane Clothing cannot get enough of drifting. The spectator seating area was packed to capacity, and these two couldn't get a seat. They had driven all the way from Southern California to the San Francisco Bay Area to watch Formula D Round 4.

(5) The award for first crash of the event (and coolest graphics) goes to Mark Arcenal from Drift Unit, who must have crashed because he was distracted by the realistic larger-than-life graphic of import supermodel Jeri Lee, spread eagle on his hood. Even when he was supposed to initiate his drift and look ahead to the next corner, he just couldn't keep his eyes off Jeri Lee. It just goes to show, women that hot are nothing but trouble.

(6) For some reason, the Charge Speed front grille on the Pacific Rim Silvia sticks out excessively, but what really makes the car stick out from the rest is the way Daijiro Yoshihara drives it. Quiet and reserved in person, Dai takes all his aggression out and expresses his true personality in the way he drives the car.

2005 Formula D Round 5: Chicago

August 6, 2005.
Soldier Field, Chicago, IL

Before the tandem elimination rounds begin, the Belle-1 sound system plays the national anthem, and just when the crowd quiets down to put their hands on their hearts, Tarzan Yamada emerges from the start area with a huge American flag waving from the window of his Team Taisan Viper Competition Coupe.

Early in his run, Hubert Young smashes the rear section of his Discount Tire S13 on the wall right in front of the audience. He gave it his all for the rest of the run, smoking his tires furiously, getting as close as he possibly can to the outside barriers to make sure he doesn't develop a fear of coming close to the wall.

Alex Pfeiffer begins his drift close to the wall with a feint and a clutch kick and controls the resulting momentum long enough to follow Conrad Grunewald through the rest of the course.

1

2

(1) Sheltered within a rollcage to stiffen the chassis and protect him in the event of a rollover, Samuel Hubinette comes wide into the right-hand sweeper, getting as close as he can to the spectators and the wall, as Conrad Grunewald closes in from the inside.

(2) Everything's bigger in Texas. Derrick Rogers from Bubba Drift gets big smoke out of his Cooper tires to the wild approval of the crowd. They loved the Knight Rider theme of the car!

People constantly complain about the air quality and smog in Los Angeles, but at least the sky isn't red. Chicago gets their first taste of Kumho's red smoke tires.

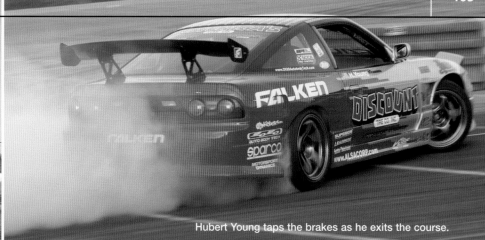

Hubert Young taps the brakes as he exits the course.

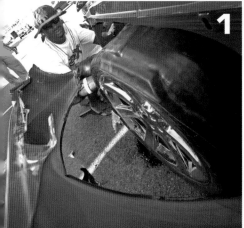

[1] Ralph Lauren male supermodel Tyson Beckford examines the damage to his Saleen Mustang in the pit area.

[2] Drift Alliance funnyman Ryan Hampton is an ex-IRL driver and driving instructor at the Bob Bondurant School of Performance Driving. Here he is pushing the suspension limits of the monstrous 1969 Chevrolet Camaro.

[3] While Carluch performs suspension surgery underneath his S13 Silvia, his friends work together to help him repair his car after he crashed it into the wall. Aside from body damage to the headlight, hood, and fender, he also broke the lower control arm, TC rod, and brake line. If it weren't for friends who were generous enough to let him borrow parts to fix his car, he wouldn't have been able to get back home to Jersey.

(4) The hood is up on Tony Angelo's rotary-powered FD3S RX7, but it's not a problem. Tony's track-support technician is Dave Gibson from Speed Machine Performance in San Diego, California, who specializes in all things rotary. While Gibson is an expert builder and tuner of Mazda RX7s, he often gets stopped at airports for his skill in designing T-shirts with clever quotes—his personal favorite is, "My drinking team has a racing problem."

Even young kids jock Falken models Courtney Day (left) and Joyce Lex (right) as they line up to get autographed post...

On the evening before the event, Soldier Field looks so peaceful with the sun setting behind the downtown Chicago cityscape.

Before heading to downtown Chicago to get pizza at Gino's East, the Pacific Rim Drift Team does some last minute tuning on Dai's S13.

Calvin Wan initiates hard into the right-hand corner in Chicago.

2005 Formula D Round 6: Irwindale
August 27, 2005.
Irwindale Speedway, Irwindale, CA

With the sun setting over Irwindale, Samuel Hubinette uses his Mopar Viper's horse-power to close in on Ken Gushi's Mustang as the pair approach the clipping point on the speedway's inner oval.

Rhys Millen uses the power of his LS1 engine to obliterate his Yokohama tires, with an abundance of smoke rolling off his Racing Hart wheels. The wheels have been customized by RMR with a fluorescent red line on the outer lip, which they used to tune the GTO's suspension at each event. RMR team manager Blair Stopnik analyzed photos and videos to figure out how much the car was leaning in different sections of the track. They used the red line on the wheel lips as a reference point to see how close the fender came to the line when the car was leaning, then used that data and tune the suspension accordingly for different tracks.

(1) Kris "Milano" Kregorian is a highly skilled driver. A former rally driver in Greece and Lebanon, Milano represents Armenian and Italian drifters. He built this green RB25DET-powered S13 coupe by himself at his own parts yard on Alpha Street, which is a row of junkyards right behind Irwindale Speedway. Milano is easy to spot at the track, just look for the brightest green car you can find with good angle and tons of tire smoke.

(2) In the middle of Signal driver Ohkubo's press interview, RMR's Blair Stopnik and Yokohama's Chad Harp sneak up on stage to give Rhys Millen a little surprise champagne bath, as Chris Forsberg and Falken model Courtney Day try to avoid getting soaked.

(3) Jim Russell racing school instructor Tony Brakohiapa partnered with male model Tyson Beckford to form Team X, which campaigned two Saleen Mustangs in the last two events in Formula D. As the two rode around the track in their golf cart, all the women who saw them became giddy. It's a hard job, but someone has to do it.

(4) The Irwindale grandstands are packed to capacity with spectators of all ages. It was difficult even to walk around to find a seat.

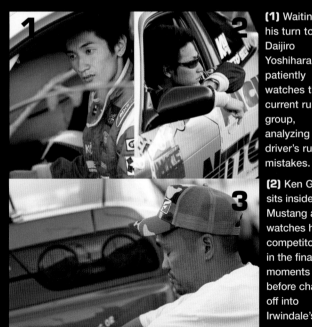

(1) Waiting for his turn to run Daijiro Yoshihara patiently watches the current run group, analyzing each driver's run for mistakes.

(2) Ken Gush sits inside his Mustang and watches his competitors run in the final moments before charging off into Irwindale's ov

(3) Robbie Nishida takes a moment to sit and concentrate on game plan before he gets into the car for his final run session.

EARLY U.S. DRIFT TEAMS

Symphonic co-founder Tsutomu (STOW-moo) Maehara's blue zenki S14 sits patiently among the amber leaves of fall on a Bay Area mountain road. This car was Tsutomu's daily driver, but he outfitted it with Bride bucket seats, Cusco roll cage, LSD, suspension, exhaust, gauges, and a Keiichi Tsuchiya steering wheel. He even picked up his mom from the airport in this car. It just goes to show, drifting is not a fad. It's a lifestyle.

THE AE86 DRIVING CLUB

Back in the late 1990s, some of my friends and I started the AE86 Driving Club. We weren't really a drift team or anything back then, but almost all the members of this club are deep in the drifting scene now. We came up with the idea one night and Calvin Wan immediately began working on designing the original sticker, which had the silhouette of an AE86 on it. (Several years later, we even discovered low-quality pirated versions of the sticker on eBay!) We met at Serramonte Macy's and Ling Nam before we even gave the club a name, but it became more official once Calvin made the sticker and we put them on our AE86S. We met up and drove together through San Francisco, screwing around on city streets and on the 280 freeway going back and forth, racing and doing dumb stuff. We raced each other with stock, 112-horsepower bluetop 4AG engines—I don't know who we were kidding.

The AE86 Driving Club was created as a group of people who liked to *drive* their AE86s, hitting all the SF Region Solo2 autocross events. I used to drive from San Jose to Daly City to meet up with Calvin and Yves, then we'd drive out to Candlestick Park, Oakland Coliseum, or even Stockton and Sacramento on 13-inch Panasports just to drive three laps, work the course, then go home. A lot of the time, it was raining, and we drove our super-low AE86s in the rain, with 13s and low-profile tires, hydroplaning everywhere. Out of our crew, Calvin was the best driver; I had all the cool parts that everyone wanted; and Yves was the best inspirational speaker—he had everyone believing that AE86s were better than Ferraris or something. A lot of my original drive and dedication to the AE86 is partly because I used to hang out with that group so often.

Unfortunately, all good things must come to an end. The AE86 Driving Club fell apart after a while, because people got busy with their lives or work, some didn't feel like driving anymore, and some moved away from the Bay. Even though the club itself fell apart, the people from the club didn't fall out of the scene completely. I ended up moving to Los Angeles, where I found a new calling in drifting

and automotive photojournalism, some of the other original members ended up linking up with other friends to become members of Northern Cali crews like Symphonic and Battle Swing. Calvin Wan ended up becoming Falken's first fully-backed U.S. works driver, and the first driver in the history of drifting to compete with a V35 Skyline/Infiniti G35, taking home the first-ever win by an import car in the Formula Drift Championship.

SYMPHONIC

Symphonic originated in the Bay Area with Victor Nomura and Tsutomu Maehara. The crew met every week in the South Bay and ran the mountain roads south of San Francisco. At the time, Calvin Wan and Dan Pina were running the mountain roads individually and later found out that they were not alone on the mountain. There was another group of cars running on the same mountain roads, and one of them, Hubert Young, had an R32 Skyline. Calvin was driving the mountains in his FD3S RX7, and he saw the Skyline on the road and was so surprised to see someone who actually drove such an expensive, exclusive car hard in the mountains!

Dan and Calvin met up with the Symphonic crew one night just to hang out, and soon began driving together regularly. Once drifting began popping up in actual venues where they could practice their skills in a safe environment, they all transferred their efforts to driving on the track and competing in professional drift competitions. Symphonic was featured in On The Scene Video's *Chasing The Touge* volume. Victor Nomura drove his AE86 to achieve a Best 8 finish at the first Video Option Ikaten at Irwindale. Dan Pina furthered his experience in road racing and autocross, and now drifts in his "Drift Patrol" Ford Mustang. Tsutomu Maehara quit his job as a sushi chef and moved to Southern California to become a team driver for Megan Racing. Calvin Wan and Hubert Young both became Falken team drivers, touring and drifting at different venues all over the United States with the Formula D Championship series.

BattleSwing/ SwingBattle

BATTLESWING

Battle Swing was a group of hardcore AE86 drivers from the Bay Area who used to get together on Friday nights and run the winding mountain roads somewhere north of San Francisco. Original members included Alex Pfeiffer, Stan Lee, Hiro Fujita, Gaylord Garcia, Ryan "Bigan," and several others.

When SpeedTrial USA started holding drift events, members of BattleSwing drove from San Francisco down to Southern Cali in a caravan of Corollas.

Since these guys were always hanging out and driving together, they thought it would be cool to form an official crew. Then one night, Hiro came up with the name out of nowhere, and says, "Hey what about BattleSwing?" The group stuck together for a long period of time, but after a while, several of the guys in the crew got out of the car scene, and some moved away.

SWINGBATTLE

When drifting started becoming more and more popular in Southern California, the frequency of drift events began increasing at an incredible rate. Alex Pfeiffer recalls spending at least two weekends a month in Southern Cali, where he became good friends with Andy Yen, a fellow AE86 driver and king of the mountain in Southern California. Together they formed a So-Cal chapter of BattleSwing, called SwingBattle.

Andy and Alex didn't want to be on the same team; they thought it should be separate because they didn't want two top drivers on the same team. So Andy linked up with a couple other So-Cal canyon runners he was friends with and brought them into the team, with the only criteria being that they needed to be fast in the canyons. The new members of SwingBattle were Chris "Chinky" Chau, Brandon Friedman, and Nick Trota. In a somewhat jokingly, but partially serious, manner, Andy explained with a smile, "I wanted to come up with a team that would be faster than Alex's."

SLIDE SQUAD
www.davescholz.com

Slide Squad was one of the first drift teams to be formed in the United States—Thousand Oaks, California, to be exact. Slide Squad's two members, Dave Scholz and Mark Hutchinson, were early pioneers of drifting in the United States who met while taking Japanese classes in college. They were into the old-school Japanese drifting scene, with mean-looking Hachirokus with Goodline front bumpers, OEM side skirts, and normal OEM rear bumpers; with TRD wings and fat-lip 14-inch wheels with demon camber and ridiculously stretched tires. They liked super low down S13s with 15-inch SSR Mark 3 wheels or Precedeo Demon Camber wheels. This was before the popularity of full aero kits; a time with only zipties, zenki lips, and Japanese team stickers all over the windows.

Mark had a "smurf blue" S13 coupe with a Silvia face and an SR20DET motor. He was the first guy in the United States with an SR-powered S13 with Silvia face for drifting, and the first who had an RB25 for drifting. Dave drove an EF Honda Civic hatchback, painted camouflage to mimic the car of famous front-wheel-drive Japanese drifter Keisuke Hatakeyama, and he put authentic Japanese team stickers all over the car. This was one of the things that set Slide Squad apart from other new groups of drifting enthusiasts in the United States. Slide Squad had all the cool authentic private team stickers.

Stickers may not seem like anything important to most racing enthusiasts, but team stickers are really core to drifting culture in Japan. Drift teams in Japan exchanged team stickers with their friends—it was something like having merit badges. When people saw team stickers on a drift car, it showed off who the owner of the car was friends with, or who they drifted with. It was even cooler to have stickers from famous or well-respected drift teams, or teams from areas of Japan that are far away from the car owner's home area. Since Dave and Mark were from the clean-cut, suburban area of Thousand Oaks, California, it was cool that they had all these real, authentic Japanese team stickers. It's not like you could just buy them somewhere. They had to be obtained from the drift teams themselves.

A motorsports maniac, Dave had been watching F1 and WRC on TV since 1993, and historic motorsports since he was a little kid. Dave originally put his website up in 1995, with mostly Japanese N1 and Super Taikyu racing photos on it. In 1996, Dave went on a trip to Japan with his brother, and visited Twin Ring Motegi Circuit.

Once he got back to Southern California, Dave met up with Mark and asked if he wanted to drive out to Little Tokyo in downtown Los Angeles and check out Japanese bookstores, since they were both learning Japanese at school. It was in Little Tokyo that they discovered untapped resources: the Yaohan Market and the Kinokuniya and Asahiya Bookstores. It was inside these bookstores that they discovered Japanese car magazines like *Option*, *Option2*, *Young Version*.

One day while on a trip to Little Tokyo, they found J-Wave Video, a place where they could rent Japanese car videos. From then on, they were hooked. They met after work on Friday nights, went down to J-Wave and rented whatever new videos they had. Eventually, they found a Japanese market in Northridge called Jet Set, which had Japanese car video rentals in the back.

By 1997, Mark and Dave were officially hooked on Option videos. Dave says they both agreed that their favorite Option segments were always towards the end of the videos, where they showed drifting! Dave recalls, "We loved watching the drifting portion

at the end of the videos. The drivers were having so much fun, drifting and messing around, doing dumb stuff like messing around with life-size cardboard cutouts of Keiichi and shit like that. It was hilarious!"

In January 1998, Mark and Dave went to the Tokyo Auto Salon with the *Turbo Magazine* tour. While Mark stayed in Tokyo with a friend, Dave took the *shinkansen* (bullet train) down to the Kansai area of Japan where he went to Rokko Mountain. Dave recalls, "I heard something that sounded like a crazy swarm of bees coming up the hill. Then suddenly, I saw this JZA70 Supra with open exhaust, ripping up the hill with R33 GTR wheels. Next was a JZX100 (turbocharged 6-cylinder Toyota 4-door sedan, which comes in 3 varieties—Chaser, Mark II, and Cresta) and a group of JZX90s (same car, but one chassis model earlier than JZX100) from this team called D-Club. All the cars were red, and then a couple months later, when I was back in [Thousand Oaks] that same car was on the cover of *Carboy!* Dude it was rad! So I called and woke up Mark back at the hotel in Tokyo to tell him about it. That's the moment I turned into a Japanese car and touge nut."

When he got back home, Dave says he was looking to experience something like this again, but there was nothing like that at all in the United States. "Then we discovered touge when me and Mark came over to your [author's] house that time," Dave explains, "Remember? We didn't even know there were mountain roads over there until you told us and took us up there. We all used to meet up with everyone at the Texaco station, and then after that we went up and used to run touge almost every Friday night Dave drove his Civic from Thousand Oaks, 200 miles round trip every weekend."

Mark is still very active in the drifting community, and constantly practices at JustDrift events. After selling his Civic, Dave ended up buying a 1972 240Z, and still drives it on the canyon roads in Southern California.

DRIFT ALLIANCE

Drift Alliance is one of the most recognized drift team names in the United States. The team includes Tony Angelo, Chris Forsberg, J. R. Gittin, and Ryan Hampton. This rowdy group of drivers from the East Coast has been stirring up a lot of attention in the Formula D circuit as members of Team Falken, with their 1980s rock-star look and rebel attitude.

The team was founded in Doylestown, Pennsylvania, as the brainchild of team member Tony Angelo. He came up with the idea of starting a drift team after noticing a BMX team called "Little Devil." Tony explains, "They weren't super well-known, but they were bad ass and had cool clothes and the best videos ever. I wanted to do the same thing with drifting. I also came up with the idea from looking at the Forum Snowboard team. It was basically started by this guy, Peter Lyon. He just kinda made his own team and did whatever he wanted. So basically DA is more about our enthusiasm for drifting than anything."

When they first started the group, they made shirts that read "ECDA," (East Coast Drift Alliance). Tony continues to recollect, "Me and Chris [Forsberg] made up the name around March 2003, maybe. Me and Chris had FCs (second-generation RX7s) and some of our friends were into Japanese anime, so they had Option videos and stuff. They also had anime friends in Japan who would email them little cartoon clips of Initial D, which we could watch on Realplayer. That was like in 1998 and 1999."

Tony and Chris knew how to do some basic fabrication, and they didn't really have much access to performance parts for their cars. They had access to a lot of engine build-up stuff, but didn't know where to go for suspension yet. So with mildly built up cars, Tony says "we just decided to go full-on drift because it was cool and reckless."

After some talking, Tony met up with his friend Matt Petty. The two told the owner of Englishtown Raceway about their idea of holding drifting events at the track. The track owner decided to let Tony and Matt put together an event.

Erik Jacobs attended the first event they had, Drift Out Wednesdays. It was held on the last Wednesday night of every month. After only two Drift Out Wednesdays events, Matt Petty was contacted by Wired Magazine, which had heard about their events, and hit them up to do an article on drifting. Petty wasn't interested, so he blew them off. However, Wired was determined, and they contacted Matt again two months later. A short time after, the magazine showed up to one of the drift practice days, and met up with the group again when they returned to Pennsylvania. Wired featured an article on Tony Angelo and his experiences starting out with drifting in the Pennsylvania backroads, and his journey out to the D1 Driver Search at Irwindale, California, in their October 2003 issue.

Tony found out about the D1 Driver Search about 18 days prior to the event, and, in typical DA gung-ho fashion, decided to do it. Tony and Chris borrowed a bunch of money from relatives and took whatever they could out of their bank accounts. They spoke to Naoki Kobayashi from Drift Association, who gave Tony and Chris his own personal registration spots, of which there were only two. The duo rented a Ryder truck, loaded up their cars, and drove across the country.

Once Tony and Chris got out to Southern California, they were amazed. "We had never even been to California before," Tony explains. "When we saw the level of the drivers in the drifting scene and support they all got from sponsors and everyone, we just felt that we could be doing this too, and we should be doing this. So we moved out to Cali. Chris got a ton of support from his family to move out. They helped him get a new 350Z, and right away he supercharged it, blew the motor and crashed it a few times. That thing had full suspension and bad-ass rims. And a real Vertex body kit." Tony came out to the West Coast to see what he could do with drifting as well. Chris moved to Long Beach and got a job working at Signal Auto. Tony went to Nor-Cal to work at a small speed shop, but things didn't work out with that, so eventually he moved back home.

Things took a turn for the better when Jarod DeAnda got in touch with Tony. He wanted to help him out and represent him. Soon after talking, Jarod hooked Tony up with Rockford Fosgate and Vivid Racing.

At the end of 2003, Tony and Chris approached Vaughn Gittin Jr. (J. R.), and asked him to be on the team. They knew JR from driving together at early DG Trials events. Tony admits, "Chris didn't think it was a great idea at first. He didn't think JR was good enough. But I thought he was totally motivated and had wicked drive. Then we asked Alex (Pfeiffer) to be in DA too, and he immediately told us about (Ryan) Hampton. Alex was telling us he was a good driver and a maniac too. So we were like, cool. Great fit."

During this time, Chris was building his 350Z at Signal Auto, and Tony came up from San Diego to help him with it. Chris had just blown his supercharged motor in his 350Z, so he thought it would be a good idea to put an SR20DET in the car because an SR was definitely less expensive than a brand new VQ engine from the Nissan dealer. Since I knew the SR-powered 350Z would be something fresh and new that American magazines hadn't seen before, I asked him if he'd be interested in doing an exclusive photo shoot with me. After some negotiating, Chris agreed, and David Pankew from Modified Magazine agreed to use my images of Chris's SR-powered 350Z on the cover of their October 2004 issue, which turned out to be one of the top selling issues for that year. That issue was the first time a Drift Alliance car had ever been on the cover of a major nationwide magazine. Tony admits "that car was always a big deal for DA. And of course Chris always did really well for DA as well."

Tony wanted to make a video ever since he got into drifting. His friends were all skaters and BMXers from the East Coast. Tony says, "We saw the import scene as totally techno-rave style and we thought it was totally lame. We couldn't relate to that. So we thought it would be cool to make a video about what we were totally into." Tony then called up his ex-college roommate, Pete Varley, and talked to him about making this video. "Pete was my roommate at Drexel (University), and he was a film major. I was in mechanical engineering." Tony explains, "So we got 16mm black & white film and did death scenes for everyone. It was cool as shit."

AMERICAN DRIFTING CULTURE AND TRENDS

U.S. Drifting DVDs and Video

JDM Insider   www.jdm-insider.com
Grip Video   www.gripvideo.com
On The Scene   www.livesockets.com
CLUB4AG Drift Review   www.driftday.com

TOWHOOK TOYS

For some reason, it has become some sort of trend for people to hang toys or other items off their cars' rear tow hook,   but the origination of this trend came from the bosozoku (street gangsters with fixed up cars) in Japan. It was a bosozoku trend to hang a small tin bucket from the rear towhook to show off how low their cars were- they got the idea from seeing cement trucks in Japan, which always had a bucket hanging off the rear of the truck. The cement trucks used the bucket as a "catch can" of sorts, so that excess cement from the truck wouldn't spill onto the pavement. Inspired by this, the bosozoku trend-setters attached small buckets to their rear towhooks to show how low the bucket could hang- if your car was so low that the bucket could scrape on things as you were driving, they thought it was cool as hell.

TEAM STICKERS AND BUMPER STICKERS

Not sponsor stickers. These are team stickers!
One of the things that set Slide Squad apart from other new groups of drifting enthusiasts in the United States were the cool, authentic private team stickers. Stickers may not seem like anything important to most racing enthusiasts, but team stickers are really core to drifting culture in Japan. Drift teams in Japan

would exchange team stickers with their friends—it was something like having merit badges. When people would see the team stickers on a drift car, it showed off who the owner of the car was friends with, or who they drifted with. It was even cooler to have stickers from famous or well-respected drift teams, or teams from areas of Japan that are far away from the car owner's home area.

Aluminum "spin-turn knobs" became popular among drifters. People unscrewed the car's factory e-brake button and removed the spring inside the handle, and replaced the original e-brake button with an aluminum spin-turn knob. By removing the spring and installing the spin-turn knob, the driver could pull up the e-brake lever and release it quickly while drifting, without getting the e-brake lever stuck in the upward (engaged) position.

Formula D star AE86 driver Taka Aono uses zipties to hold his front bumper corners to the fender. They're easy to fasten, lightweight, strong, and convenient.

ZIPTIES

Forget nuts and bolts! Zipties (also called cable ties) are the number-one choice of fasteners used in the world of drifting! Without a doubt, if you went to a drift event and asked people their opinion on what the quickest, most convenient way of securing a bumper to a car would be, 8 out of 10 people would probably answer, "zipties!"

Why you ask? They are strong, lightweight, easy to carry, inexpensive, and easy to work with. These are all the factors that drifters value!

In drifting, people often replace their OEM bumpers with fiberglass or carbon fiber aftermarket aero kits. These aero kits are getting more and more aggressive as drifting styles become more developed. When a car's body work gets damaged in a drifting accident, zipties are essential! Drifters are often able to repair their cars and attach bumpers to fenders, and other body parts just using zipties. Most drifters always have zipties in their cars.

APPAREL

Making custom drifting apparel is something uniquely American in nature. In Japan, the drifting related T-shirts people wear are more like shirts with sponsor logos. In theUnited States, people have customized their own shirts with their own graphics or messages.

PACIFIC RIM

Founded in 1996 in San Marino, California, by Jerry Tsai, Pacific Rim Apparel is the first name in automotive apparel, and a benchmark in the import car industry. Shortly before he started Pacific Rim, Jerry came to the realization that there weren't any real clothing brands for people into import cars. At the time, most of the people in his age group were rocking mainstream brands that definitely did not represent the drifting lifestyle. "What about clothing for people who love cars?" Jerry voiced his concerns to his brother, who then suggested that Jerry take on the task himself. From that point, Jerry realized he wanted to give the automotive aftermarket lifestyle its own type of clothing.

Jerry started out with only three designs in 1996, selling the shirts to Southern California car shops. By the end of 1996, Jerry launched the Pacific Rim website www.iloveracing.com, but he wasn't able to take orders until 1997. Jerry explains, "E-commerce technology didn't really kick in until around that time, so it was hard for me to start at first".

In 1998, he went to Japan with his friend Ken Miyoshi to check out some parking lot car shows. They visited a place called "The Check Shop" in Yokohama and "Red Rine Racing" (Japanese for Red Line Racing) in Chiba, and they started selling his shirt.

In 2002, Jerry traveled to Japan again, and had a booth at the X5 (Cross 5) Car Show, where he sold T-shirts. Cross 5 is like Japan's version of Hot Import Nights. After the show, Jerry got some help cleaning up the booth from a new friend that he met there— Daijiro Yoshihara.

At the time, Jerry had no thoughts of starting a drift team. Daijiro wasn't even a recognized driver in Japan or the United States; he was just a normal guy attending a car show, who drifted in the mountains for fun. In fact, it wasn't until 2003, when he heard that D1 was coming to the United States, that Jerry decided to start up a team. Jerry explains, "I wanted to participate in drifting. I wanted to represent that we're an American-based clothing company, but with a Japanese driver.

Nowadays, Jerry focuses his efforts on running the Pacific Rim Drift Team, and campaigns his S13 Silvia in the Formula D series, with Daijiro Yoshihara as the pilot. Since the drift team competes at all the Formula Drift events, Jerry always has a Pacific Rim Apparel booth at all events, focusing on clothing, stickers, and other cool drifting-related gear. Jerry's online sales are mostly from U.S. customers, but he has received quite a few orders from other countries, such as Canada, the United Kingdom, France, Germany, Japan, Singapore, Australia, New Zealand, Dubai, Bahrain, Argentina, and even the Middle East.

DRIFTWELL

Driftwell was founded by Herb Policarpio in Los Angeles, California. A drifting enthusiast himself, Herb saw that drifting was starting to grow and recognized the opportunity to create an apparel company to complement the sport. In 2003, Herb started giving out stickers to friends and selling Driftwell t-shirts, trucker hats, and other items out of the trunk of his AE86 at Drift Day events. Driftwell started out as an underground phenomenon on the West Coast, but is now worn by drifting enthusiasts all over the United States. It also has been popping up in worldwide media outlets like *Super Street*, *Import Racer*, *C16 Magazine*, *Autoweek*, *LA AutoGuide*, *Modified Magazine*, *D-Car*, KCAL9 TV Los Angeles, and Formula D TV on G4 Television.

Ashley Sarto hanging out at the Pacific Rim booth in her Pac Rim "Girl Racer" boybeater tanktop. 2005 Formula D Round 5, Chicago, Illinois.

While planning out run groups with Yoshie Shuyama, Kenshiro Gushi is sporting Pacific Rim's "Hooked on LSD" shirt at Drift Showoff Miami.

Thai Marie Cali rocking the Pacific Rim "Drifter Groupie" baby tee. Photo courtesy Jerry Tsai

CIPHER GARAGE

The Cipher Garage Clothing was started by people with a passion for AE86s and "86 Life," a term coined to describe the lifestyle built around the cars and drifting culture. Cipher Garage takes inspiration from everything loved about AE86s, drifting culture, and 1970s/1980s era "Japanese muscle cars"—cars with negative offset wheels, drift team stickers, stretched tires, vintage steering wheels, and carburetors. Cipher Garage's designers incorporate these iconic images of drifting culture and blend it with stylish color combinations and graphics to appeal to the fashionable set, which also has an appreciation of graffiti and sneaker fashion.

TOKYO DRIVE

Having designers both in Tokyo's high fashion district of Harajuku and Los Angeles, Tokyo Drive is a cross cultural clothing brand that caters to the drifting market. It draws inspiration from historic Japanese drifting culture, along with up and coming American drifting culture.   Tokyo Drive sponsors world famous drift team, Team Orange.

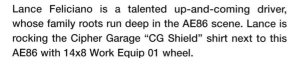

Lance Feliciano is a talented up-and-coming driver, whose family roots run deep in the AE86 scene. Lance is rocking the Cipher Garage "CG Shield" shirt next to this AE86 with 14x8 Work Equip 01 wheel.

(above) **Mark Sanchez** has a very clean 1973 Corolla in the garage, but he can't stop drifting with his turbocharged AE86 Levin coupe. He is shown here rocking the Cipher Garage "Offset is Everything" shirt.

(right) **Charlene Guerrero** making her fresh-fitted "CG Collection" tanktop look hot.

SHIKANE CLOTHING
Schikane Clothing was founded in 2002, by Jay Yoshida, Bill Shew, and Tobin Honda, from Los Angeles, California. It is fashion inspired by the underground street scene of Los Angeles and the founders' passion for drifting. Schikane's goal is to increase people's awareness about the lifestyle that is being created by young and fashionable car enthusiasts. Pooling resources with other automotive clothing lines, Schikane partnered with a group of like-minded designers to produce the Fashion Icons Show, the first-ever runway fashion show for the automotive apparel industry. With high profile events like this, Schikane has certainly been doing their part to raise the bar of the automotive apparel industry.

SPEEDWELL SHOES
Speedwell Shoes was a brand of racing shoes that catered to the growing market segment involved in drifting.

Tobin Honda and Charlene Guerrero rocking Schikane Clothing, a Los Angeles–based clothing brand that focuses on drifting and the L.A. street scene.

Popular San Francisco–based designer Mark Arcenal created Drift Unit, a Bay Area clothing brand that incorporates graffiti and sneaker culture elements into clothing design, corresponding to his popular websites (www.driftunit.com and www.fatlace.com) , which present drifting photos and information in a stylish manner.

Speedwell shoes were first introduced to the drifting and go-karting markets by former employee and Formula D announcer Jarod DeAnda.

Speedwell found a new boost of energy in John Pangalinan, who worked to revamp the shoe lineup and colorways to turn Speedwell into more of a "racing lifestyle" brand. John created a custom shoe for Samuel Hubinette, the First Series Champion of the Formula Drift Championship, and signed drifting prodigy Ken Gushi shortly after.

Pangalinan and Speedwell later collaborated with Jerry Tsai of Pacific Rim Apparel, making Speedwell the first shoe company to offer custom-made driving shoes in special colorways to suit each sponsored team, somewhat like "basketball court" shoes (think Michael Jordan and Shaquille O'Neal) for their sponsored drivers. With new Pacific Rim Drift Team edition, Ken Gushi edition, and Samuel Hubinette "Toxic Drift" edition driving shoes catering to drifters, Speedwell started a strong new marketing campaign focusing on the company's involvement

Outfitted in pink Speedwell racing boots and a short skirt, Thai Marie Cali certainly drew attention to Speedwell's booth at Formula D Round 6, reinforcing the idea that racing shoes are cool to wear.

with top drift stars, import icons, and top import models. The magazine ads and event marketing through Hot Import Nights car shows and Formula Drift events seemed successful in building the company's brand, but unfortunately, the company closed down in January 2006 because the owner suddenly decided to go in a different direction with his finances.

The First Race Queens: Umbrella Girls in Drifting

Yokohama Tires umbrella girl Junisa Kim holds up traffic at the start line as she stands next to Rhys Millen's Pontiac GTO. 2005 Formula D Round Irwindale Speedway, Irwindale, California.

D1 Grand Prix umbrella girl Leah Dizon at D1 Grand Prix February 2005. Irwindale Speedway, Irwindale, California.

Wow. Falken Tires umbrella girl Joyce Lex at 2004 Formula D Round 3. Infineon Raceway, Sonoma, California.

Team Falken umbrella girls(left to right) Veronica Becerra, Joyce Lex, Courtney Day at D1 Grand Prix February 2005.

Cars for Drifting in the U.S.

CAR CHOICE AND PREP

To properly prepare a car for drifting, it is necessary to first choose the right kind of car. Most drifting enthusiasts prefer to use front-engine, rear-wheel-drive (FR) cars for drifting because of the basic layout and weight balance. It is not absolutely necessary to have a front-engine vehicle for drifting, as it is possible to drift in mid-engine, rear-wheel-drive (MR) cars, such as the Toyota MR2, Acura NSX, and rear-engine, rear-wheel-drive (RR) platforms, such as the Porsche 911 and the Volkswagen Beetle.

FR IS BETTER

Most drifters prefer the FR layout because the majority of the engine's weight is in the front of the car, making for more responsive steering input. This also allows for a relatively lightweight rear end, which is useful for kicking the tail section of the car around.

While it may be easier to kick the tail out on a car with a heavy rear end (MR or RR), it is more difficult to recover and control the drift because the lack of weight over the front wheels will cause understeer. Also, the concentration of weight in the rear makes it easier for the car to rotate (spin) when in a condition of oversteer. This being said, FR cars are most popular for drifting, and it is quite common to see groups of FR Corollas, 240SXs, RX7s, 350Zs, early Supras, and even Miatas on track at grassroots drift events.

Two of the most popular cars for drifting in the USA are currently the 1984–1987 Toyota Corolla (AE86) and the 1988–1993 Nissan 240SX (S13). This is due to the low initial purchase price.

AE86 AND S13

It's hard to put an average price on these cars, because prices vary greatly depending on the condition of the vehicle and the location. It used to be possible to buy a good-condition stock Corolla GT-S for around $1,000 on the used market, but the prices have skyrocketed in recent years, and nowadays it is difficult to find a decent-condition car in Southern California for under $4,000. However, it is still possible to find the cars at low prices in other states, especially if the sellers aren't aware of the car's popularity among cult drifting fans. The same can be said of the 240SX. The prices of S13s and S14s have been going up steadily as the gospel of drifting spreads across the country, as new drifting fans scoop up all the used cars out there, then crash them.

Both the AE86 and 240SX (S13 and S14) have developed a large fan following among drifting enthusiasts, as a large percentage of celebrity drivers in the Japanese drifting world prefer the AE86 or 240SX for drifting.

The AE86 and the S13 are both excellent platforms for a basic multi-purpose vehicle to be used for drifting, road race, or autocross events, while maintaining street-driving functionality. While either car can be enjoyable for motorsports use in stock form, the addition of an aftermarket limited slip differential (LSD) is an absolute necessity for a serious drift car. The LSD alone will make a dramatic change in the handling and overall feel of the car. While certain models of the AE86 Corolla GT-S came with limited slip differentials from the Toyota factory, only the HICAS models of the 240SX had factory LSD, and these HICAS models were not available in the U.S. market.

HOOKED ON LSD

It is widely preferred by most enthusiasts to use aftermarket clutch-type, four-pinion LSDs for drifting—most OEM limited-slip differentials have only two pinion gears, and tend to be less predictable and more difficult to control. Several aftermarket manufacturers (Kaaz, Cusco, and TRD) make four-pinion, clutch-type LSDs that are perfect for drifting use. Most drifters prefer to use these clutch-type LSDs instead of helical-gear-type (torsen) LSDs, due to quicker response, greater adjustability, smoother power distribution, aggressive feel, and ease of rebuilding. Since these LSDs have several metal clutch discs on the outside of the four pinion gears, it is possible to adjust the LSD's locking rate by rearranging the clutches. It is also very important to choose a limited slip with large clutch plates and a high number of clutch discs to optimize power transfer to the ground. Another advantage of the clutch-type LSD is that it can be rebuilt easily and inexpensively. If a clutch-type LSD breaks, all the clutch discs safely remain inside the heat-treated steel LSD case, whereas the torsen-type LSDs have been known to cause much more damage when broken. It is not uncommon for a broken helical gear to shatter, inflicting damage to the differential's ring and pinion gears, splitting open the LSD case itself. Furthermore, professional drifters prefer clutch-type LSDs because they provide better traction on bumpy surfaces, which is very important for most drifters in Japan, who commonly practice on deserted canyon roads and mountainsides during midnight practice sessions. If a drifter encounters a bump on a mountain pass that puts one of the drive wheels in the air, the torsen-type LSD behaves just like an open differential, which can become very unpredictable and dangerous for the driver and the car.

MONEY INVOLVED?

As with any motorsports activity, drifting is expensive, and can be as hard on the wallet as one allows it to be. It's no secret that racing is an addiction that can only be cured by poverty. Most of the money spent on the setup and maintenance of drift cars is on tires. Many amateurs start off with the idea that they should use any old tires that they can find for the rear, since they are just going to be burned up. While cheap, used tires might be OK for beginners doing donuts around

pylons, it is strongly suggested that drivers improve tire selection as their skill level improves. The cheap bargain-bin tires that worked well for doing donuts could turn out to be extremely hazardous and unsafe for advanced, high-speed maneuvers. Therefore, many drifters seek a combination of good grip, stiff sidewalls, and affordability when buying tires. Frequent drifters can end up replacing tires several times a month!

It is important to always bring tools to practice events, along with the extra rims and tires. Due to the constant high revving of the engines and demands on the transmission and differential, it is recommended that drifters change their engine, transmission, and LSD oil more frequently to avoid substantial wear and tear. Many drifters add oil coolers, aluminum radiators, electric fans, and aerodynamic front bumpers or hoods to help keep their engines cool. As with normal racing activities, racing seats, four-point harnesses, roll cages, and other safety equipment are also recommended. There are myriads of different car setups, and each is dependent on the driver's preference and budget. At the end of the day, it still all boils down to the skill of the driver.

Is FF Drifting Really Drifting?

There is a lot of controversy over whether or not front-engine, front-wheel-drive (FF) drifting cars can actually drift. While it is possible to get the car into a state of oversteer (more simply, get it sideways), many people argue that it isn't really drifting because FF cars cannot use traditional FR drifting techniques, which depend on using the power and torque of the rear wheels (shift lock, upshift, clutch kick, power oversteer, etc.) to induce drift.

However, FF cars *can* initiate drift using braking techniques (e-brake, trailbraking) and weight-transfer techniques (Scandinavian flick/short feint); shifting and clutch techniques like upshifting and clutch kick *won't* help a driver who's trying to initiate drift in an FF car. To perform an FF drift, drivers must enter the corner really hot (faster than normal), letting the car's weight transfer to the outermost tires, then suddenly yank the e-brake lever to upset traction in the rear. The driver then counter steers while keeping their foot on the gas pedal, and the car goes in the direction in which it is pointed. To keep the car's tail sliding for a long period of time, the driver must repeatedly yank the e-brake lever, locking up the rear wheels to keep the tires sliding and the car's tail dragging along.

Even though getting an FF car to oversteer is possible, to hold the drift for a long time, like what's possible with FR cars, will be very difficult. The FF car can only slide as long as the inertia carries the car when the weight is transferred. Once the inertia from the initial weight transfer is lost, then the car will straighten out, following whatever direction the front wheels are pointed.

While some say that FF sliding is, in fact, drifting, quite a few disagree. Some say that since the drivers are just dragging the rear end of the car around, it shouldn't be considered drifting at all

However, what do you tell people like Keisuke Hatakeyama, who is well known in Japan for "drifting" in his EF Honda Civic? Hatakeyama entered drifting competitions in Japan using his signature camouflage EF Honda Civic hatchback. He also tried entering events driving an AE86, but he became more popular driving the Civic, as it stood out from the crowd. People loved to see him make his little EF Civic emulate the drifting styles of FR cars with long slides and even side-to-side swaying.

While FF drifting isn't expected to become huge in the United States, the groundwork has been laid by drivers like Hatakeyama, who have inspired others to practice FF drifting, like Dave Scholz of Slide Squad and Kyle Arai from Hawaii.

Dave Slide Squad was the first FF drifter who was pretty good at FF drifting. In the late 1990s, he constantly ran the mountain roads in Southern California, swinging his tail out in a spray-painted camouflage EF Civic hatchback. He sold that car a while ago to finance a trip to Japan, so I believe his days of drifting FF cars are over. On the other hand, Kyle Arai from Hawaii drifts with a red EF Civic four-door and is pretty good. Oddly enough, he won a controversial first place at the 2005 Drift Showoff in Hawaii. While Kyle aggressively bombed into the turns super fast, many argued, "FFs cannot drift!" Whatever the case, it's up to you to form your own opinion.

DRIFTING TECHNIQUES EXPLAINED

Special thanks to Calvin Wan for his invaluable insight and driving expertise in putting together this section of the book.

Drifting is a style or technique of driving in which a vehicle is intentionally driven in a state of oversteer. The drift is induced by the driver's ability to transfer the car's weight so that the rear tires break traction. The driver then maneuvers the car completely sideways at high speed *before* the apex of the turn. The objective is to slide into the corner at high speed, setting up the car so it is already pointed correctly once it reaches the exit of the turn.

THROTTLE INITIATIONS
POWER OVERSTEER

A driver can use the power oversteer technique by turning into the corner while applying heavy pressure on the accelerator, so the rear wheels break traction and the car slides (oversteers) while going through the turn. While the driver can use this technique in any rear-wheel-drive car, it is more commonly practiced on those with higher horsepower.

LIFT THROTTLE
In Japanese drifting videos, the Drift King, Keiichi Tsuchiya, refers to this technique as "Kansei Drift." When performing a lift throttle drift, the driver shifts the weight balance of the car by using the car's speed together with throttle input to initiate the drift. The driver accelerates into the turn at high speed,

then lifts off the throttle pedal while turning in to the corner (transferring weight of the car forward) to create oversteer, then accelerates again, modulating both throttle and steering input to maintain the momentum of the drift.

BRAKING INITIATIONS
SIDE BRAKE (E-Brake)

When most beginners think of initiating drift, the first thing that naturally comes to mind is to yank on the side brake, or emergency brake.

This technique is performed by pulling up on the emergency brake lever while turning into the corner. This locks up the rear wheels, creating a condition of oversteer. Depressing the clutch pedal while simultaneously pulling up on the e-brake will momentarily disengage the engine's power to the rear wheels, allowing the e-brake to lock up the wheels more easily.

BRAKING DRIFT (Trail Braking)
Primarily used for medium to lower speed turns, this is a more advanced method of inducing drift. The driver purposely comes into the turn hotter than normal; braking late while turning in to the corner to shift the car's weight to the outermost-front tire. The weight shifting combined with the vehicle's entry speed initiates loss of traction to the rear wheels. As the rear wheels break traction, the driver counter steers into the turn and modulates the throttle input to control the car's momentum.

STEERING INITIATIONS
FEINT
While this is a rather advanced drifting technique, it is a maneuver traditionally used by rally drivers to negotiate sharp turns. However, in the rally world, the drivers refer to the feint technique as "the Scandinavian Flick."

The feint initiation is used in tight corners where a deeper drift angle is needed to clear the corner. This technique is performed by initiating drift in the *opposite* direction of the turn, then quickly rotating the car back around (into the direction of the corner) so the car oversteers into the turn at an extreme angle, using the centrifugal force of the car's rear end to whip the tail end from one direction to the other.

CLUTCH INITIATIONS
CLUTCH KICK
This technique is performed by depressing and releasing the clutch pedal while under constant throttle (the driver keeps on the gas pedal while kicking the clutch pedal). This allows the engine's rpm to rise quickly, which abruptly jolts the drivetrain, suddenly increasing the wheel speed to break traction, while turning into the corner to create oversteer.

GEAR SHIFTING INITIATIONS
UPSHIFT
To perform an upshift-induced drift, the driver enters the corner at speed, simultaneously shifting into a higher gear while turning in to the corner. This instantly accelerates the speed of the rear wheels, spinning them to break traction, while the driver modulates the steering and gas pedal input to control the drift.

SHIFT LOCK (Downshift)
The driver performs the shift lock technique by depressing the clutch pedal while turning in to a corner, allowing the rpm to drop while downshifting, then quickly releasing the clutch pedal to engage the lower gear. This sends an instant shock through the transmission, engine, and driveline components, abruptly slowing down the speed of the rear tires to induce drift. Obviously, this technique puts a lot of strain on the transmission and driveline components, so it should be practiced with caution.

DRIFTING TUTORIAL
BY CALVIN WAN

PHYSICS OF DRIFTING
Initiation techniques are listed in order of difficulty. Later techniques are more advanced.

ACCELERATING INITIATIONS
Oversteer is induced by abrupt acceleration of rear-wheel speed to break traction.
Power Oversteer
Clutch Kick
Upshift

DECELERATING INITIATIONS
Oversteer is induced by abrupt deceleration of the rear-wheel speed to break traction.
E-Brake
Shift Lock

WEIGHT TRANSFER INITIATIONS
Oversteer is induced by transferring the weight of the car to break traction.
Trail Brake
Feint
Lift Throttle

INITIATION POINT
Different initiation techniques can be used depending on where you want to start your drift.

EARLY INITIATIONS
These techniques are used to initiate drift **before** "turn in."
E-Brake
Clutch Kick
Feint

TURN-IN INITIATIONS
These techniques are used to initiate drift **at** "turn in."
Power Oversteer
Trailbrake
Shift Lock
Upshift
Lift Throttle

CONTROLLING THE DRIFT
OK, now that you know how to get the car sideways, how do you control it? There are a few things to think about.

BALANCE POINT
When drifting, it is the goal of the driver to reach the car's balance point—the state in which the car stabilizes in a drift. At the balance point, only minimal steering and throttle modulation are necessary to maintain the state of drift.

STEERING MODULATION
Turning into the corner while drifting will create an increase in drift angle. Turning away from the corner while drifting will cause the car to straighten out more, lessening the angle.

THROTTLE MODULATION
Applying more throttle will increase the amount of drift angle. Applying less throttle will decrease the amount of drift angle.

FOOT BRAKE MODULATION
The brake pedal can be used mid-drift to slow down the speed of the car. It can also be used to tighten up the driving line and to increase drift angle. If the car is already in a state of drift, stepping on the brake pedal will slow down the car, thus shifting weight to the front of the car, making the car's tail rotate increasing the drift angle.

CLUTCH MODULATION
The clutch kick technique can be used to gain momentum and speed, extend the drift, and adjust for more drift angle. The *abruptness* of the clutch kick can be controlled by the amount the clutch pedal is depressed and the duration it is held in, along with the amount of throttle used; the clutch pedal does not necessarily need to be depressed all the way to the floor. Sometimes drivers will need to kick the clutch several times, which is an especially common practice on lower horsepower cars, to gain more speed while continually breaking traction.

E-BRAKE MODULATION
While this technique is a popular form of initiation, the e-brake is not only used to induce drift. Skilled drifters also modulate their use of the e-brake lever mid-drift to hold or adjust the desired drift angle, to extend the length of the drift, and to control the speed of the drift.

ADVANCED DRIFTING TECHNIQUES

MANJI (PENDULUMS)
Drivers use this technique to maintain a drift on straightaways. This technique is performed by swinging the car's tail from left to right (like the pendulum of a clock) multiple times on a straight.

FOUR-WHEEL LOCK UP
An advanced technique used to decelerate in drift while sliding outward, widening the driving line and holding the desired drift angle. To perform a four-wheel lock up, the driver locks up all four wheels at the same time, using the foot brake and e-brake lever simultaneously.

Acknowledgments

RESPECT DUE.
My sincere and heartfelt thanks go out to everyone who has influenced me, inspired me, and helped me get where I am today. You have made this book possible.

God. Thank you for this opportunity and for taking care of me along the way.

My Parents. Especially my Mom, who would have preferred that I had gone into selling real estate instead of "wasting all my time taking photos of drifting." If I learned anything at all from you, it is that I can be successful at anything, as long as I work hard and put God first. It seems your talks have actually made some impact and inspired me to do something productive with my love of drifting. Thanks for all the advice and prayers.

My little brother Dave. My number one fan and supporter. Your unconditional love and support means the world to me. You always got my back, and I appreciate it all. I'll never forget how your eyes lit up with excitement the first time I took you to the track, and you saw drifting for the first time. It's always more pure through the eyes of a child. Never lose that enthusiasm. Every single shot, every single struggle I had to overcome making this book, every single painful step at the end of each day on every track, is for you.

Uncle Ed, for always believing in me and being supportive, no matter what. Thank you.

Kenta Ogawara, who started my career of shooting photos for car magazines by accident, talking me into ditching work so I could shoot a cover feature for a Japanese magazine! If it weren't for you, I might have never started shooting drifting professionally. Good job Kenta! (I might have gotten rich doing something else!) But several years, several plane trips, and countless covers later, I'm so glad you talked me into calling in sick.

Most people don't think like you do. Your motivation and entrepreneurial vision have shifted the way I think about life-instead of wasting your life working a job you don't care about, it's better to spend every single day of the week working hard at something you're truly passionate about, and enjoy every single day of your life.

My inside knowledge of Japanese drifting culture is all because of you. It was a privilege to work with you on all the top Japanese magazines, especially *Battle Magazine*! *BM* was so legendary and instrumental in shaping Japanese drifting culture—it was an honor to be a part of it. Traveling all over Japan with you to shoot drifting was hella dope. Let's keep pushing on and moving forward; travel everywhere we want to travel, and drive everywhere we want to drive. We can do it. This is just the beginning. Kyodai mitai na shinyuu desu.

Nick Fousekis, for all the support throughout the years. You have created so much opportunity for so many people in the drifting world. People don't always realize how much impact a single person can have on the lives of others, but because of *your* support of drifters and drifting, people like *me* have been able chase our dreams and be successful at it. You have my utmost respect and gratitude. Serious bro. This book would not be possible if it were not for you. Thank you so much, Nick.

Nobushige Kumakubo, a drifting pioneer and legend who has become family to me. You are the heart and soul of drifting. We used to watch you drive your *borohachi* (haha gomen ne!) in old drifting video tapes and magazines, but never in my life would I have dreamed that I could be close friends with a person like you. You have opened my eyes to the world of drifting in Japan and inspired me to share it with others.

From the very first moment I set foot on the legendary Ebisu Circuit, it was like a religious experience. One of my favorite quotes is "Life is not about how many breaths you take, but the moments that take your breath away." I can't forget the last night on my first trip to Ebisu, when I stayed up all night to take pictures of the drifters at Harumatsuri. I will always remember watching the sun rise that day, over the trees at South Course, with the sounds of spooling turbos, wastegates, and screeching tires. It was music to my ears. It took my breath away. Ebisu truly is *The Holy Land of Drifting*. Thank you for introducing me to your mountain. Ebisu has captured a piece of my heart forever.

Calvin Wan, a true friend who has been with me every step of the way in my quest to document drifting. When we started out as a bunch of Bay Area kids screwing around driving our AE86s, who would have ever thought that drifting would make it this far? Your determination to become successful as a professional driver has inspired me to keep focused, too. Thank you so much for all the technical help in the Drifting Techniques section of the book, and for being there for the whole journey as we both grew up with this new motorsport.

Jeff Yip, who helped me when I was launching my career. As a photojournalist, your professionalism is impeccable and an example I've always tried to follow. Thank you for always supporting me and my photography.

Yasutaka Ogasawara, my photography sempai. Thank you for advising me when I was starting my photography career. After talking to you, I'm always inspired to try harder and never stop shooting.

Lomax, for being a huge supporter of my photography, and more importantly, my mission. Thanks for being down.

Jose and Ericka Gonzalez, my Miami family. Thanks for always having my back, and more importantly, for the yucca frita and croquetas from Versailles and La Carreta.

Jennifer Johnson, Peter Bodensteiner, **Jim Michels,** and MBI. Special thanks to Jen!

WORD UP.
Good looking out to those who have helped me on my journey to create this book. (To any I may have forgotten, my deepest apologies.)

Herb Policarpio, Ippei Tahira, Meriel Rafanan, Ken and Hatsumi Miyoshi, Mark Arcenal, VIPete Ulatan, Kota Desu, The Ogawara family (my family in Tokyo), Auntie Agnes, Pia, Koichi Mori, Fred Inocencio, Jamm Aquino, Jerry Tsai, Ricky Silverio, Patrick Ng, Arnell Benitez, Anthony Lazo, Donald Shrum, Tem Wu, Rodel Cantillon, Tobin Honda, Charlene Guerrero, "Ojichan" Jay and the Yoshida brothers, Stan Tran from NBC Universal, Kelvin Tohar, Jay and Joyce, Chris Neprasch, Phillip Velasco and Robby Abaya from 360 Video, Ronnie and Justin, Steve Starr, Tiny Panganiban, Dave and Mark SlideSquad, Toshi Matsui, Scott Toshima, Reiko Ige John Guiliani, Rodney Wills, Kazuhiro Tanaka, Naoto Suenaga (nisemono Masao!), the real Masao Suenaga, Mitsuteru Igusa (korosozo bokeh), Akio-chan, Yu-kun, Robbie Nishida, Shinji Minowa, Charlie Tyson, Yamashita Koichi, Shigeru Ohki, Ryuji Miki (koara ni niteru), Hoshino, Minami, Kazuya Bai, Shinya, Takahiro Ueno, Ken Maeda, Toshiki Yoshioka (50 Cent), Gushi-san, Mama, Hikaru, Ken Gushi, KC, Toshiki, Dai Yoshihara, the entire Falken family, Darren Thomas, Mr. Honda, Mickey Andrade, Mary Pilcher, Tree Feierday, Yasuhiro Nozu, Taku Machida, Josh Spears, Anthony, G-Hatt, Stretch, Tim, J-Brad, Zach Siglow, Steve Heuer, Josh Krane, Robert Juster, Deb McBride, G4 Television, Belle 1 Brothers, Clayton York, Art Michalik, Kristina Lew, Chad Harp, Yokohama Tire, Maxxis Tire, Cooper Tire, Toshi Hayama, Joyce Lex, Courtney Day, Mercedes Terrell, Eri Moriyama, Veronica Becerra, Sunisa Kim, Thai Marie Cali, Lea Lam, Ainsley Hyman, Verena Mei, Stephen and Mayumi Dietrich, Kero One (aka Byungjyo), Job and Titus Hammond, Dan Stampf, Henry Duong, Erik Jacobs, Tom Carter, Greg and Nito Labrador, Paul Umholtz, Royce Fujimoto, Justin Kikkawa, Lincoln Chee, Ryan Naka, Cindy and Carrie Sato, Steve Oliberos, Farid Herschend, Steve Jimenez, John Amador, HPI Racing, White Warren G, Marlon, Sonny, Revo, James Bondurant, Gary McKinney, Henry Chung, Hubert Young, Hiro Sumida, Taka Aono, Al Lagura, Gabe Tyler, Andy Yen, Andy Sapp, Alex Pfeiffer, Crystal Dominguez, Kent Chen, Samuel Hubinette and Stina, Lance Feliciano, Ross Petty and Colleen, Gene Jasper, Conrad Grunewald, J. R. Gittin, Chris Forsberg, Tony Angelo, Ryan Hampton, Jarod DeAnda, the Hamachi Bros., Bryan Norris, Tommy Chen, Ray Nakadate, Sajee, Jeremy Sakioka, Tsuyoshi Inoue, Masa Goda, Steve Nakamura, Mark and Erin Sanchez, Bill Murphy, Javier Paramo, Booney Renfield, Chris Overley, Casper and Pat Monstor, Blake Fuller, Milano, Damien Takahashi, Sharon Luv, Shin Masumori, Jay Lapid and Graphtech Stickers, John Pangilinan, Wally Seto, Jenice Yu, Jason Tse, Kevin Tidwell, Adam Matthews, George Ciordas, Harry and Hannu, Chris and Diana, Karlo and Mark, Greg Taniguchi, Adam Saruwatari, Chris Rado, Makoto Yokoo, Kawasaki at Drift Tengoku, Takahashi at *Battle Magazine*, John Naderi, Jonathan Wong, *Super Street*, David Wallens and *GRM*, Soichi Kageyama and *Daytona Magazine*, David Pankew, Joe Magro, Naoki Hiratsuka, Ben Ellis, Curt Dupriez, Tim Downs, Mike Van Horn, Keith Buglewicz, Jared Holstein, Jay Canter, Jason Siu, Craig Taguchi, Mike Maez, Alison Merion, Fly of MaxPower, Courtney from GR8, Christophe, Pete Varley, Victor Carillo, John Pangalinan, Steve Bitanga, Toshio Noguchi, Yasu and Yu, Thuy Dang and Live Sockets, Dave and Mike from Grip Video, James Louis, Apex'i USA, Jim Chaparas, Carol McConnaughey, Allison Lopez, Edwin Nunez, Andy Williamson, Steve Levy, Julian Wait from FHM, ESPN, Todd Christensen, Blair Stopnik, Eric Cantore, Rhys Millen, Scott Dodgion, Eric Knappenberger, Shari McCullough, Darren Jacobs, Rusty Blackwell, Eddie Alterman, Mike Mucklin, Cindy Lam, Julian One, Brian Urbano, Brian LaFuente, Dalton Hanley, Mike Ramsaran, Juan Henao, Sam Chang, Sam Jspec, Richard Barzaghi, Edgar Garrote, Arnold Escano, AutoPlus, Tito Solis, the Collantes family, the Cabral family, Cir Sayoc, Yves and John, Benson, Avon Bellamy, Steve Mears, Maurice Smith, Ken Ebo, Dele Atanda, Tony Brakohiapa, Eric Haze NYC, Tyson Beckford, Moto, Naoki, all Drift Association volunteers, Formula Drift, DG Trials, Drifting.com, everyone on Club4AG, TORC, TRD USA, my AE86 friends worldwide (too many to name), people on CipherGarage's Myspace, my Miami crew, and my family at Ebisu.

Last but not least, my heroes. This goes out to the original hardcore teams of street drifters who drove their cars into battle night after night, whether it be at *touge, futou,* or circuit. You are my motivation and inspiration. Rough World, Running Free, Caution, Tielaps Club, Hey Man, DP2, Bross Running Crazy, DropOut Racing, Eightysix Factory, T50 Japan, NA Works, Oto-kichi Family, Coasters, Tinker, ICBM, Drift Ensemble, Rapid, GunTama R, Response Family/Sessions, After Fire. Break, Lock On, Night Walkers, Marionette, Premier, Vivien, Kumakazoku, Futou Noki, Peak, Slide Squad, BattleSwing, SwingBattle, FNR, and Geki Kassou Dan.

Speed Secrets: Professional Race Driving Techniques

ISBN 0-7603-0518-8

Inner Speed Secrets

ISBN 0-7603-0834-9

Speed Secrets 5: The Complete Driver

ISBN 0-7603-2289-9

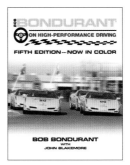

Bob Bondurant on High-Performance Driving

ISBN 0-7603-1550-7

The Fast and the Furious: Official Car Guide

ISBN 0-7603-2568-5

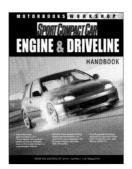

Sport Compact: Engines and Drivelines

ISBN 0-7603-1636-8